LOVE
BUSINESS
MARRIAGE

FOREWORD BY
REY BERMUDEZ

LOVE
BUSINESS
MARRIAGE

VISIONARY AUTHOR

TAMARA MITCHELL-DAVIS

Love, Business and Marriage

Copyright © 2023 Tamara Mitchell-Davis.

All rights reserved. No part of this book may be reproduced in any form or by any electronic or mechanical means, including information storage and retrieval system, without written permission from the author, except for the use of brief quotations in a book review.

Published by CEO Wife Publishing
www.theceowife.com

Unless otherwise indicated, Bible quotations are from the Holy Bible, King James Version. All rights reserved

Scriptures marked NIV are taken from New International Version ®. Copyright © 1973, 1978, 1984, 2011 by Biblica, Inc. ™
All rights reserved

New Edition lyric written by James Harris III and Terry Lewis for MCA Records, December 1988.

The stories in this book reflect each author's recollection of events. Some names, locations, and identifying characteristics have been changed to protect the privacy of those depicted.

Manuscript editing
Heather Asiyanbi
www.pensandproof.com

Book Creation and Design
Ellese & Co Creative
www.elleseandco.com

ISBN for Paperback: 978-1-7375400-6-9
ISBN for E-Book: 978-1-7375400-7-6
Library of Congress Control Number: 2022923345

DEDICATION

I dedicate this book to the couples who have faced challenges in their marriage and those that may find themselves within the words of these stories.

MARRIAGE IS WORK

Throughout this book you get a glimpse into real life experiences told from both the husband and wife point of view. Learning to love, forgive, rebuild and restore: love, business and marriage.

TABLE OF CONTENTS

Foreword ix
    Rey Bermudez

From Bankrupt To Building Wealth 3
    Catherine Latoya Grant-Alston

Establishing A Business Mindset After Bankruptcy 15
    Reginald Alston Jr.

Business And Love: You Can Have Both 27
    Tangie McDougald

Standing Firm In My Manhood
And Getting Out Of My Own Way 37
    Kyle McDougald

When The Honeymoon Is Over, Stick And Stay! 49
    Lashonda Wofford

Sacrifices You Make For Love 61
    Travis Wofford

Pay To Play! **73**
   Dr. Sh'nai Simmons

Just Like God Planned **85**
   Min. Taiwan Simmons

Second Time Around **99**
   Tamara Mitchell-Davis

A Changed Man **109**
   Joe Davis

Guided Reflections **121**

Meet the Authors **131**

Foreword
REY BERMUDEZ

Think of the last couple you watched dancing harmoniously together on TV or in person. What captivated you the most? Were they incredibly smooth or could you see the passion in their moves? The commitment in their attitude? Or was it the example of their partnership? Whatever the reason, you were captivated with the unity of their performance and how they carried out effective communication. You would probably use the words beautiful, amazing, or sexy. Maybe you even wished to be just like them.

But what got them there? Yes, some people are born dancers, but no one is born to dance perfectly with someone else. No one sees the countless hours of practice spent over the years that go into the seemingly perfect performances. No one sees the let downs and disappointments as a result of conflict and tension. Very few have experienced the behind-the-scenes or how unexpected challenges interfere with and slow progress. It is that perfect moment in time, the snapshot of a three- to four-minute dance everyone appreciates and celebrates, not the work it took to accomplish it. The same can be said of successful healthy marriages.

As a trained counselor and master teaching artist, I have the unique opportunity to see the dance of marriage play out on and off the dance floor. From the first steps of connection to the passion of performance to the comfort of routine, couples are constantly negotiating the varying rhythms of togetherness while navigating the pain of stepping on each other's toes. Ouch! I also enjoy the blessings of rewritten narratives, the rekindling of desire, and the renewal of mind leading to oneness in marriage. I have the honor of witnessing the couple determined to see marriage as a covenant over a contract, to dance as one, completing and complimenting each other in and through their faith in God. Tamara and Joe are one of these couples.

When Tamara asked me to write the foreword for this book, I was both excited and humbled. Ever since I've known Tamara, she has held a passion for sharing her lived experience with the hope of encouraging others. It certainly ignited a new chapter in her marriage and business. Her calling to service has expanded to include the authentic representation of women and marriages from everyday walks of life, and her desire to inspire intentional conversations led to transformed and thriving relationships, something she now shares with Joe.

Love, Business, and Marriage adds to the collection of strategies and possible answers for both partners in marriage seeking new steps in the dance of managing how to best prioritize their relationship while managing home and a business. With resources like the stories told in this book, my wife and I become more polished dancers every day that passes. What the couples teach us in their chapters is how to balance the obvious challenges and learned benefits of marriage: greater fulfillment, clear KPI's (key performance indicators) and eternal ROI's (return on investment) glorifying the One. Tamara has put together a collection of writers with messages of hope that are critical when fewer than one in five Americans see marriage as essential for living a fulfilled life. Post pandemic, could you imagine what the numbers are now?

What you will read in the pages of this book gives you the opportunity to go behind the curtain with a few couples to experience their dance as it pertains to love, business, and marriage. You'll come to understand the steps that were taken or missed and the moves that were made or failed. In particular, the undeniable power of faith, hope, love and mutual submission to God that led to imperfect harmony while encouraging the next generation of couples to do better. You are not reading a manual on do's and don'ts. Rather, personal narratives to learn by example, as opposed to the hard edge of experience to hopefully inspire and transform your marriage dance for many years to come. This is the moment to show the world that second chances are worth it, marriage is worth it, and a legacy of healed, healthy communities to come is worth it.

Leave room for discovery and have fun!

Rey Bermudez
Relational Dance Specialist & Counselor

Connect with Rey at:
www.steps2one.com
Rey@relationaldance.com

#TEAM ALSTON

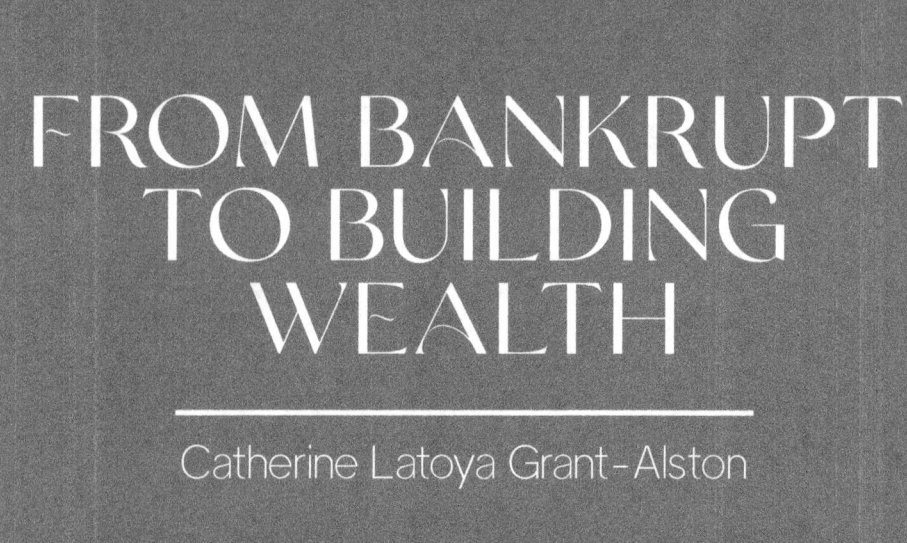

FROM BANKRUPT TO BUILDING WEALTH

Catherine Latoya Grant-Alston

FROM BANKRUPT
TO BUILDING WEALTH

Catherine Latoya Grant-Alston

Be willing to be uncomfortable. Be comfortable being uncomfortable. It may get tough, but it's a small price to pay for living a dream - Peter McWilliams

As I sat at the kitchen table, hand still on the phone shaking, all I could think was, "Oh, my God, what has happened?"

I immediately broke down in tears. I cried so hard, I was hyperventilating and could not catch my breath. A million things went through my head, but what I remember most was that a $50 bill was pushing us past the breaking point.

I knew it was only a matter of time before Reggie, my king, would be home and I would have to explain what happened. When the king came home, the look on my face told him that something was terribly wrong. As he walked into the kitchen and put his laptop bag down, he said, "Queen, what is wrong?"

My eyes began to swell up with tears again as I fumbled with the words to say my credit score had dropped because of a $50 medical bill. I called the credit collector to ask them if I paid the $50 would they just remove the bill from my credit report. It didn't matter how much I pleaded with them, they stated that they would not remove the bill. They said that if I paid, they would report it as paid but it would still have to remain on my credit report.

Our credit scores were the last piece of our financial stability. I apologized over and over. I tried to keep everything together. I tried to keep everything afloat. I failed us! The king looked at me and told me not to cry. He told me everything would be okay. He hugged me as I sobbed all over his white button-down shirt and bowtie.

That day in August 2014 is so vivid in my mind because it was the day that we had to admit we were spiraling down financially. That $50 bill was what made up our mind to give it all up and file for bankruptcy. By January 2015, we finalized our bankruptcy. Walking out of that courthouse felt like a relief, but at the same time, I felt like the ultimate failure. How could I, the financial guru, the individual who had been working in banking since I was 16, be in a position to file for bankruptcy? How could I, the individual who kept a credit score of 730+ since the age of 18, file for bankruptcy? I was in disbelief! All I could think and imagine was that we had hit rock bottom with no point of return.

Let me talk to you about how we got there. The interesting thing about hitting that ultimate low wasn't a matter of mismanaging money.

In 2009, I decided I was going to get my MBA. Because I received credit for many of the classes I took while obtaining my Bachelors of Science in Business Administration from the University of Connecticut, I was only required to take 11 courses to obtain my graduate degree. I already had student loans, and I accumulated another $45,000 in grad school. A year later, in just a matter of months in 2010, we purchased our first home and also had our first child. What we did not anticipate was the difficulties I had during the pregnancy. Multiple hospital stays and bedrest became the norm for the nine months carrying our princess. After our baby girl was born, we looked at our financial situation, and we determined that I could stay home with her without having to return to work. Having one parent working and the other at home can be very rewarding and a strain at the same time. I was at home and instrumental in all her milestone developments, providing for and protecting the well-being of our baby. But we also had only one income.

After staying home for a little over a year, I wanted to go back to work. We had started receiving the medical bills from all of the hospital stays, and we also wanted to ensure that we had some residual income to do things such as go on vacations, participate in hobbies, and participate in my sorority and Reggie's fraternity. We also felt that it would provide us with some financial freedom. I went back to work at a corporate institution and our princess stayed with Grandpa. They were the ultimate buddies and we loved having the support.

In 2012, the princess started daycare. We didn't qualify for any assistance because of our incomes. Therefore, we paid full price for daycare. If you know anything about daycare pricing, you know it is extremely expensive. At the time, we were paying $250 per week, on a monthly basis. Daycare was almost as much as our mortgage. In essence, a portion of my income was immediately consumed by the daycare obligation. However, working in corporate America afforded me a nice salary that more than covered the daycare bill. Medical bills were manageable. Student loan payments were manageable as well. We took at least one family vacation per year. The king and I also enjoyed multiple weekend stays away to recharge our marriage. We were doing fairly well.

That all changed in November 2012. One morning when I was proceeding down the stairs to iron my clothes for work, I slipped and fell. I fell down the stairs and hit my head on every single step going down. The next thing I knew was my husband holding me and asking me if I could hear him. I remember telling him I could. He assured me that everything would be OK and that the ambulance was on its way. Unbeknownst to me, I had a seizure. I had no idea what had transpired. All I knew was that I fell down the stairs.

I remember getting to the hospital and being in the emergency room with two doctors and a full team of nurses and staff looking at me. They cut my hoodie off, and I was in a neck brace. One doctor was cutting my bra off and I begged her not to do it. Now if you know anything about being a very voluptuous, top-heavy woman, then you know a good bra is very difficult to find. I had on my good bra that day. You know the bra that costs almost $100 that keeps the girls up and looking like a teenager? Yeah, that bra! I definitely did not want them to cut off my bra. The other doctor completely understood what I meant. I remember the two doctors going back and forth about protocol versus reality and so forth. Ultimately, they simply removed it. When I asked where my husband was, no one had an answer for me. The one thing that I knew about my king was that he would never leave me alone in a situation like this. I began to panic. The doctors started asking me to sign papers and requesting consent to treat me, and I said I wasn't doing anything until my husband was there. When the king finally came in, he reassured me that everything would be okay.

What I didn't know was that they were holding my husband and restricting him from coming to me. He was questioned about pushing me or harming me. Once I started questioning and asking for him, and the fact that he got our lawyer involved, they finally let him come in. After numerous scans and tests, it was revealed that I had suffered a brain injury and had contusions all over my chest and ribs from the fall. I lost my short-term memory and had to attend rehab for over a month and a half.

We had a long road ahead. As you can imagine, an emergency room visit, hospital stays, and a month of rehabilitation cost us significantly.

The king and I had a newfound outlook on life. There was no way that we went through something so traumatic that we would come out and not be grateful. Although we had the additional medical bills, we still elected to be grateful for every single day. Before my injury, we decided to have a second child. Our princess was almost three and we thought it was an ideal time. We had already started trying to conceive, but we were not successful. After rehab and the recovery from the fall, we decided that we would give it one more shot. Lo and behold, I found out we were expecting. The king was excited, and his happiness made me feel that everything would be okay. In November of 2013, we welcomed our prince into this world.

However, of the nine months I was pregnant, I was on bed rest for five. Many hospital visits and overnight stays created additional medical bills. Although I was working and had adequate insurance coverage we still had to pay deductibles and copays. After delivering our son,

I had to stay in the hospital a few additional days because of high blood pressure from preeclampsia. We expected this because it had happened with our first baby, but nothing can prepare you to be away from your newborn. Unlike with our little girl, this time around I wasn't staying at home with the children. I had to go back to work with two children under the age of four. I'm most grateful for my grandparents who assisted us on a daily basis. Our prince was able to stay home with my Grandpa for eight months. But our boy was growing and moving at a pace faster than any of us anticipated. Because he was growing so fast and my grandpa was aging (73 years young at the time), we decided it was best to start the prince in daycare.

The medical bills had been piling up since before our son was born. We had already set up as many payment plans as we could with the various hospitals, surgeons, and doctor offices, but the bills just kept coming and coming and coming. It became extremely overwhelming. We literally had over $40,000 or so in medical bills. We were also paying student loans, car notes, and our mortgage plus daycare for two kids. Our daycare bill per month was more than our mortgage payment. How insane is that? Even without our mortgage, we were well over $100,000 in debt. The reality was that we did not mismanage our money; life just got in the way. For about two months we tried our best to stay above water, but the day I received the collection notice for $50 changed everything.

Going through bankruptcy was a learning experience. It was also humbling. As much as I knew about finances, it definitely changed my opinion and the stereotype I held about people who filed bankruptcy. So many times you think that people who file bankruptcy overextended themselves and mismanaged their money. But that's not the case in our scenario. That's actually not the case for many people who file bankruptcy.

I was meticulous with our budget. I had a great credit score and was never late on any payments. Ultimately, though, I was in a position where I felt like I had to choose between feeding my family or having childcare. What we found was that filing for bankruptcy was not the end of the world. We did not lose our home nor did we lose our vehicles because we had an outstanding payment history; instead of being forced to sell our home or give back our cars, we were allowed to choose how we wanted to handle them. What bankruptcy did for us was alleviate the medical bills and the credit card debt we used trying to stay afloat. Also, because you can't charge off student loans, we still have those.

Our credit scores took a major tank. We went from 730+ to a score in the low 540s. However, seven years after filing, we had a trust for our children and family. Yes, that's right we have trust fund babies. We built a portfolio that is going to provide wealth for generations. We purchased a larger house and even purchased and sold a rental property for a profit. We have assets totaling over $1 million. Yup, you heard that right, we are millionaires. Of course, it didn't happen overnight. It took work! With determination and supporting each other, we were able to climb out of what we considered the bottom to rise and reach for the stars.

Of course the million dollar question is, how did we do it? I'm glad you asked!

We created a plan and we stuck to it. We would pivot when necessary but not deviate from the goal. The goal was to rebuild a financial portfolio that was stable and from there, create generational wealth. We traded nights out with the friends in the club to money date night, a term we use to describe time set aside for the king and I to review our finances to ensure that we stay on track. We bring our wine and whiskey and enjoy each other's company at the same time we're reviewing our current situation and planning for our future.

We had friends who were not happy with the fact that we were not hanging out, but it was more important for us to rebuild. They didn't know what we were going through financially. Not many people knew that we had filed bankruptcy. As a matter of fact, as I write this, I can tell you that even my closest family members were not aware. We were embarrassed!

As we rebuilt our financial foundation, we were also encouraged to build something greater and more profound for our children. Out of this determination was born the Alston Kingdom, a social lifestyle brand that provides financial coaching to small businesses about using automation so they can spend less time looking at numbers and more time building their business. What people don't know is that you can't have a booming business and a busted life. Therefore, we also provide financial coaching to individuals through our Kingdom Wealth Journey course. We know what it feels like to rebuild your financial portfolio from nothing to a million+.

I encourage anyone who is having financial difficulties or who has gone through hardship in the past to look at the situation as a lesson. The experience is meant to build you to be greater. Although it may not seem like it at the time, there's always a lesson. Take these trials and turn them into a testimony. Building up from the lowest financial point of bankruptcy taught us some critical lessons. Most importantly, it allowed us to understand the financial struggle and appreciate walking with Kingdom families through hardships. Here are some financial tips that you can take with you and use in your Kingdom like we did to rebuild our financial portfolio.

First, know your numbers. Often, we look at our bank statements or transactions but really don't know cumulative amounts of spending. For example, do you know how much you spend eating out each month? Do you know how much you spend on gas? If your answer to any of these questions was, "I believe I spend around ...," then you don't know your numbers. The best way to know your numbers is by having a budget. Creating a budget will help you know what you should be spending. Tracking your spending against that budget will let you know if you're truly spending that amount, more or less. Creating a budget and knowing your numbers is the foundation of any financial plan. Here's a tip for my business folks: your business also needs a budget! It doesn't matter what stage of the game you're in, this is the first step so that you can continue to build wealth.

Second, make sure you communicate within your kingdom. The king and I knew we were in a tough financial situation because of all of the medical bills, the daycare costs, and everything else in between just to maintain life. However, it wasn't until after we finalized the bankruptcy that we started sitting down and reviewing the budget together. Money date night allows us to communicate. We're so busy living our day-to-day lives, passing by each other because of our busy schedules, kids sports, and all the other obligations that communication can be tough. Gaps in understanding can happen simply because of the lack of time that you're together. It's imperative to create that time and foster those habits so that you can continue to build. Alston Kingdom runs money date nights periodically so be sure to connect with us if this is something you're interested in learning more about.

Third, determine the goals of your kingdom. It's so important that you are aligned with what you would like to accomplish. Maybe the queen is looking to save for a vacation, but the king is looking to save for a sports car. Maybe you're both on the same wavelength for purchasing a house within a certain amount of time. Before you can build and implement any type of plan, you need to have the same overarching goals and similar timelines. This is crucial to the next step in the process.

Fourth, implement a plan. Once you determine your kingdom goals, implement a plan. That plan should consist of the goal, the timeline, and the milestones necessary to accomplish the tasks. What does that look like? Here's an example: Implementing a plan to be credit card free within two years. The milestones would be listed as contributing a certain amount of money every month to each credit card. You also would list each credit card in chronological order for payoff. That's a solid plan to implement based on your goal of paying off credit card debt.

Last, remain committed. Life will throw so many different challenges at you. Yes, we remain flexible, but even in those times, it's more important to remain committed. Sometimes your plan may not go just as detailed as you mapped out, however the end goal remains the same. The commitment to obtain that goal must remain intact. It's so important to remain committed because once you deviate from the plan for a month or a year, it takes that much more time to obtain the goal. Staying committed means motivating each other and your kingdom. I know that can be more easily said than done. Even after the bankruptcy, I experienced three more surgeries, including heart surgery. The medical bills started again, but this time, we were prepared. We had a plan, so we could pivot accordingly. Trust me, remaining committed and focused is the key to your success.

I hope you take these financial tips and create a plan to start building wealth. I hope that hearing my story will let you know that you are not alone. My wish is that you relieve yourself of any shame and guilt from past decisions.

Many people, especially those deemed successful, carry so much guilt and shame about financial decisions. I'm here to tell you to release that guilt and grant yourself some grace. I carried guilt for a very long time about my health issues and the financial impact it had on our marriage and our kingdom. The king would always tell me that God would make a way even when I didn't see it. His positivity, even in those dark times, pushed and motivated me. Sometimes, having encouragement and support is more important than the actions that you take.

I'm truly grateful that from the tears I cried at the kitchen table to the time I'm writing this chapter, the king has been extremely supportive along the way. Even if you don't have the support that I did, encourage yourself to keep going because if we can do it, then you can as well. Keep striving and building your kingdoms! We need more millionaire and billionaire kingdoms in this world!

REFLECTIONS

REFLECTIONS

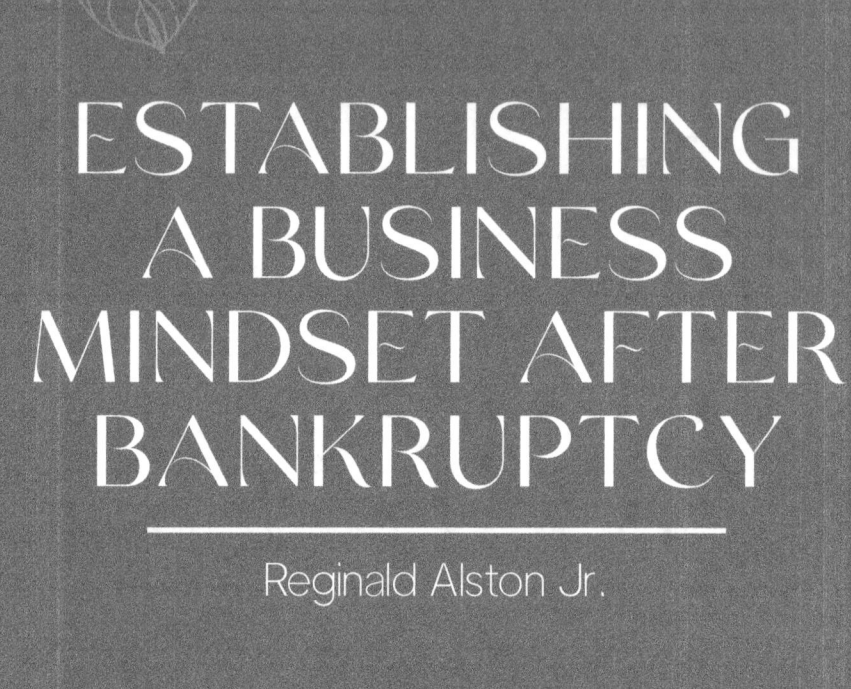

ESTABLISHING A BUSINESS MINDSET AFTER BANKRUPTCY

Reginald Alston Jr.

ESTABLISHING A BUSINESS MINDSET AFTER BANKRUPTCY

Reginald Alston Jr.

"Treat your marriage like your bank account, always deposit into it or else it will go negative." - King Reggie Alston Jr.

Hello Kings and Queens, my name is Reginald Alston Jr., and I am the King of Alston Kingdom. What is Alston Kingdom? It's a lifestyle brand that promotes Black love, Black wealth, Black excellence, and everything in between. Now that you've been introduced to Alston Kingdom, let me give you some insight into the king, or Uncle Reg as I am known to most. I grew up in New Haven, Connecticut, also known as The Elm City. I was raised in a multi-family home that my grandfather owned. We lived upstairs, and he rented out the lower level. It was located on the toughest street in New Haven, but to me, it was home. Growing up in The Elm City wasn't without its challenges and I must thank all the positive male figures in my life; my grandfather, stepfather, uncles, and more.

I believe it was this collection of men that helped me understand how to become a man and process my emotions. They taught me the values of challenging myself, holding myself accountable, how to overcome adversity, how to win, and how to deal with loss. It wasn't until I was a married man that I truly understood how the lessons about losing and winning would impact my life.

I met my lovely wife, the Queen, Mrs. Catherine Grant-Alston, in college. We dated for a few years, and in 2010, we got married, bought a house, and had our first child. We also had decent jobs. You would think we lived the American dream. You'd be wrong.

Most people would think that would be enough for one year but not us. We were living life, and life came at us fast. We were hit with a multitude of medical issues, rising childcare costs, and the unexpected need to care for loved ones, and it all led to bankruptcy.

That's right. BANKRUPTCY.

How did we get there and what did we do to overcome our situation to start a business that focuses on financial literacy? Bankruptcy is something I would have never considered because it meant I didn't know how to handle my money or wasn't being responsible with my decisions. I felt like I could never talk to my children about money again or anyone for that matter. I told myself to get my shit together, but the truth is, bankruptcy took a lot of weight off our shoulders. It wasn't an easy choice to file for bankruptcy protection, and doing so comes with obligations like attending mandatory courses on financial literacy and making better financial decisions.

Point 1:
The one question I get asked the most is how we can own a financial literacy business and have a bankruptcy on our record. Isn't that a contradiction? The short answer is no, because from a business perspective, the Queen and I had everything together. We did not grow as quickly as we would have liked, but our business practices were sound. Most credit card companies keep personal credit cards and business credit cards completely separate, and we leveraged that loophole. Additionally, when it comes to filing for bankruptcy there are different reasons for filing and different types of bankruptcy. It wasn't until I was able to sit down with a lawyer that I truly understood all the different and valid reasons for bankruptcy. What I learned through the process was that you can recover from bankruptcy quickly if you have the correct mindset and make the correct moves.

What I also learned was that NO ONE WANTS TO DEAL WITH YOU! ALL the credit card companies were like, nope, we're good on you. You get labeled as a high-risk borrower, or worse, put on the unofficial list of blackballed customers. The lesser-known credit card companies reached out to us, the ones that aren't tied to banks or credit unions, otherwise known as credit card resellers. Translation: these cards come with high interest and low balance availability. My recommendation is to STAY AWAY from these credit cards. It looks good at first because traditional credit card companies won't deal with you, but be patient. It will turn around.

Point 2:
We live in a world of NOW and YESTERDAY. No one wants to be patient and truly earn it anymore. I remember telling myself to use the cash I had on hand and if I didn't have it, then I didn't need it. Then I received the junk mail offers of pre-approvals, and you will, too. But keep this in mind: if those lenders are willing to work with you after a bankruptcy, others will follow. If you continue good banking and spending habits, even the most stubborn lender will come around.

Point 3:
You and your partner have to be aligned. For those of you who are single, divorced or widowed, I would say you and your internal voice have to be aligned. If you are not totally committed to getting back on track, then you've already lost. My Queen and I made sure that after we filed for bankruptcy and took the necessary classes, we would never end up in this situation again. We asked ourselves a very important question: "How is it that our business is in good shape, but our personal finances got out of whack?" Once we asked ourselves and each other this question, we looked at things differently. We started to approach things differently and looked at things with a business mindset. Once we unlocked this key approach, we stayed aligned with our goals, values, and vision on how to move our finances forward. Out of this very simple question came money date night when we discussed how much money went out for the month versus how much money came in. We discussed up and coming expenses such as family trips, birthdays, car maintenance, and taxes. We had a system to track our money and to help ensure that we knew what our monthly expenses were versus ad hoc expenses.

Using the business mindset also helped us approach our marriage differently and look at some aspects of our marriage as a business. We held board meetings to talk about how our marriage was doing according to the stockholders. We provided one another evaluations stating where we thought the other was successful and where there was room for improvement. We gave one another bonuses in the form of gifts or coupons to be cashed in later. Practicing the business mindset in our marriage allowed us to use safe words for when we were angry and couldn't receive what was being said to us at the time. Leveraging the business mindset made us extremely accountable and helped our marriage grow.

Who knew that filing bankruptcy would have this type of impact on my (our) life? I, for one, knew bankruptcy would change my life but not in a way that would bring my wife and I even closer than we were. It seemed like we dug ourselves into a hole with medical expenses and trying to meet everyone else's expectations for us. We had to figure out how to get back to daylight on our own.

Point 4:
When you've got it, everyone needs it and wants it, but when you've fallen in the mud, trying to get clean is all on you. I sit here writing this, saying I truly do not have one regret helping my family. The only issue I had was I felt that the same energy we gave to family should have been reciprocated and it wasn't. The lesson learned was to put my wife and children first and then help those outside my home.

Point 5:
After filing for bankruptcy, I had to take ownership and ensure that past mistakes would not repeat themselves. I had to take a hard look in the mirror and own my shit. It was said to me once that real men put away excuses, so I put away all the excuses about filing for bankruptcy. I started instead to leverage the business mindset and properly plan for my (our) future to avoid another piss poor performance.

Point 6:
Expect that the only thing constant is change. When you come out of filing bankruptcy, you have a few moments of reflection, which is natural, and then you go to one extreme or the other. Meaning, either you spend like crazy what money you do have, or you save like crazy and spend too little. The key is to find that balance. We found our balance through money date nights by understanding how our finances worked and identifying the strains that contributed to the bankruptcy. Once I understood how our personal finances truly worked versus

assuming how our personal finances worked, it was a complete game changer. Now that's not to say just because you know how your personal finances work, you are all set. There are always curveballs that will be thrown your way, but truly understanding your personal finances plays a major role in how you handle those changes.

Point 7:
Getting back on track requires work, and sometimes that work is hard and frustrating. If you stay with it and stay disciplined, then you will see the light at the end of the tunnel. Bankruptcy has a lot of negative connotations with it, but following a sound plan will make all the difference. If you filed for bankruptcy, you have to let it go and move on to start the process toward reestablishing your credit, reestablishing your financial literacy, reestablishing your worthiness for lenders, and moving from what some may view as a negative chapter in your life. The queen and I took the negative connotation of bankruptcy and turned it into a learning opportunity for ourselves. We took this opportunity to look at what we were doing right with our business and applying that to our personal lives and our personal finances. Establishing that business mindset made all the difference in the world, and I encourage you to find your version of a business mindset and execute on your plan, whatever that plan may be. One of my key success factors was having a partner that was truly supportive and was able to understand this wasn't a her or an I issue; it was a collective Team Alston issue. We both were onboard with getting back on track and we had the same collective goals, which made it extremely easy to follow a plan and execute on a unified vision.

In conclusion, going through the bankruptcy process allowed for a level of self-reflection that I only received one other time in my life. The bankruptcy allowed for me, not only as a king, but as the king of a Kingdom to reflect on areas of opportunity, where there were areas for me to be a stronger leader, and where there were areas for me to strengthen my companion. Statistically speaking and according to marketwatch.com, financial hardships and disagreements over money are one of the top reasons why marriages end in divorce. I am thankful, we were able to work on and through our financial hardships together.

I would like to take this time to thank my wife for being such an amazing partner through this financial recovery process. I also need to thank my financial literacy coach for keeping me on track and my attorney for highlighting how we could reestablish and expedite repairing our credit throughout the bankruptcy process. These key individuals, along with a host of others, aided in our full recovery and bounce back. It is only through this small village and tight knit circle that I am standing before you today as a king who can truly say his bankruptcy journey is only a small footnote in what is turning out to be a phenomenal journey. I'll leave you with this, our biggest mistake in life is that we don't dream big enough and that we're too afraid to fall or stumble. As long as you get back up, dust yourself off, and keep pushing forward, you, too, can and will have a life of abundance.

Marketwatch: https://www.marketwatch.com/story/this-common-behavior-is-the-no-1-predictor-of-whether-youll-get-divorced-2018-01-10.

REFLECTIONS

REFLECTIONS

REFLECTIONS

#TEAM MCDOUGALD

BUSINESS AND LOVE: YOU CAN HAVE BOTH

Tangie McDougald

BUSINESS AND LOVE: YOU CAN HAVE BOTH

Tangie McDougald

No Matter Where You're From, Your Dreams Are Valid ~Lupita Nyong'o

"Getting it out the mud," is an understatement.

If I had to identify a great role model in life, I must give a huge shout out to my mother, Sandra L. Richardson. She raised six children—three boys and three girls—single handedly. The most profound moments in my life consist of my mom teaching us about God, working hard to provide for us, and instilling family values and traditions. I was in elementary school when I started my first business selling penny candies and coconut ices for 25 cents out of our kitchen. I didn't understand then, but today I get it. I was learning the value of the dollar and how to hustle to get customers. Because my competition was the neighborhood ice cream trucks, I had to be consistent, offer bigger portions, and have something that the ice cream trucks didn't have to stay in business. I had to add value, so we extended our business hours and sold double scoops of Baskin-Robbins ice cream with a sugar cone for 75 cents. Mr. Frosty's single portion waffle cone sold for $1. Business was booming, and our home was known as the ice cream house.

I have always been a big dreamer and always envisioned myself as married, owning a home, having children, a dog, and a white picket fence. Yes, my dream was a replica of what most would consider the American Dream, and it was instilled in me when I was a little girl. If you had these things, it was assumed that you'd made it in life. So, when I became a teen mom, there was a part of me that paused. The ice cream business came to a halt. Friendships ended. Time felt as if it was frozen, and the world counted me out. Life was stacked against me as an unwed single mother, but I had to figure it out. I disappointed so many people by dropping out of high school and having to find a full-time job. I wanted to prove to the world, but most importantly to my mom, that I could handle being a teen mom. I couldn't fold. I had one kid while she made motherhood look so easy juggling the responsibility of six children. My mind was on a mission to be the best mother and provider despite my inexperience with being a parent. Nothing would stop me from living out the American Dream. I can't say I worked hard at finding a life partner, and I will admit that I was more vulnerable because settling down and getting married was the "right thing to do." So, I did.

There I was at the tender age of 24, married with three children, and by the age of 27, some of my other dreams had come true. We had several dogs, and I even purchased a home and installed a white picket fence. Yes, I had finally made it.

"Momma, I made it!" I silently yelled to myself.

I have lived out what I envisioned as the American Dream by beating the stereotype of teenage motherhood. I sat there thinking my mission was accomplished, but there was so much missing in my life. I struggled to hold onto a marriage that was unhealthy, but I had to keep it together in order to keep my dream alive, I would remind myself. There was an aura of darkness that hid behind my smile. Eventually, my dreams told me I deserved more and outweighed what I thought was a perfectly imperfect fit for me. My new dreams replayed constantly in my head, and I grew restless and often daydreamed, doodling on paper and trying to figure it all out. My dream included me loving myself even if it meant being by myself, of going back to school and furthering my education, and of owning my own business. Some judged my journey and said, "I had it all." After all, I had a good paying job, children, and a man that loved me. Family members whispered that I was selfish to leave and stupid to start all over. Not knowing what the days would bring, I did just that. I chose me.

It was my 32nd birthday, and I'd been Googling how to file for divorce. I was tired of it. I realized that the life I was living was superficial. It looked pretty on the outside, but it had all types of mechanical failures brewing on the inside. My life was built on a rocky foundation forged from what I thought life should look like. It afforded me a lot of tangible things that allowed me to mask the deficits my soul yearned to be filled.

Although I didn't want to admit it at the time and even as I write today, I realize that the company I kept and some relations had a negative impact on the decisions I made. I had to learn what it meant to protect my space. The reality is we don't get to choose our family, the people we grew up around, or even those who grew up with us as family. Even when relationships are unhealthy, there is a piece of us that yearns for our loved ones, the good, the bad, and the ugly. I had to learn to love from a distance, but it took me years to get into that space. In the meantime, I found myself embedded in negativity and naysayers. Once I understood that protecting my space did not mean I fell out of love or like with family or friends, I could still build boundaries, set limitations, and show people how I wanted to be treated all from a distance. I guess you could say I was finding myself.

Not long after my divorce was final, and as I was figuring out how to love myself, I struggled with the fact that another man (my current husband) loved me. Everything about him was the opposite of my ex-husband. It all seemed to be happening so fast.

I struggled with what love and support looked like in a healthy relationship. I finally had a voice, and it was important to keep it. So, when I was met with differences in our current relationship, I had to learn how to work through them and not fight because of them. This was not something that was easy. Heck, I still struggle with it today. Truth be told, my past experiences serve as a reminder that I am worthy to be in a healthy relationship and remind me to assess my current situation and determine whether it's worth fighting over.

Learning to love myself only expanded my ability to dream big. I now dream of abundance. I think I have always had the mindset to live big, but it was suppressed while I lived in an unhealthy relationship. I could only see as far as what I was taught success looked like and that was a particular version of the American Dream. Once I chose myself, the skies opened in front of me, and I felt reborn. I learned how to breathe, walk, and even talk differently. There was so much inside of me that lay dormant for so long that my physical appearance even evolved. I heard remarks like, "There is something about you that's changed," or "You have this glow that brightens up a room." I lost well over 40 pounds of weight that had been holding me back from pursuing my dreams.

When I met my current husband, we both had a vision and desire to become entrepreneurs. He remains my biggest cheerleader. We tried several business ventures to become successful, but we always fell short. For a long time, I blamed our failure on our differences in business styles. My husband's business approach is more informal while my approach is quite the opposite. However, there are lots of companies that are successful using multiple and/or complex business models. Therefore, I had to learn how to stop trying to change him and take ownership of the things I could control and my own actions. I had to examine what were the true challenges that were blocking my success and what I needed in order to push past them. Now let's be clear, this was not an overnight epiphany that I decided to look at myself. It was starting a clothing store, a convenience store, a yard clean-up business, and a snow removal company that all failed and made me say, "Enough." I had to question myself and ask, "What am I doing wrong?" and "What part of the business failures belong to me?" There were a few things that came up for me, and I had to face the hard truth.

I subconsciously self-sabotaged my success. Yes, what was happening in my personal life was also a factor in my professional life. Even though I could envision success and I believed I would be successful, I had a hard time accepting the fact that I deserved to be successful. I was raised in the 'hood' where I can't count one person who made it out successfully. Actually, the way out for my peers was either jail, drugs, or death. So me wanting more out of life and truly feeling I deserved it were too different things. I just knew that I wanted to prove wrong those who counted me out, to show them being a teen mom did not mean I had a death sentence. It did not mean my life had to stop. But I kept hitting a wall. I struggled with having a life partner and being submissive for the sake of unity. It was easier for me to operate from a dysfunctional lens than from a lens of simplicity. So, if my husband said turn left, I turned right. I frustrated him, but it didn't make a difference to me. I was causing fires, and I could not stop them from spreading. For the sake of my own ego, I was happy to let them burn, even if it meant taking business losses.

Of course, I never identified any of the failures as my own. I was so far gone; I couldn't smell the shit in my own backyard. One would think after losing so much with each other that we would call it quits, if not with the relationship, at least quit with doing business together. But the eagerness to win was there and so was love. This was all so confusing to me. I wanted to win but didn't understand what was happening. I felt trapped. As a mental health therapist, I felt I had nowhere to turn. I had to get naked and bare myself to see the barriers that were blocking my success. After a lot of soul searching, the answer was in my face. I had been using one of the most common defense mechanisms but had overlooked it: the fight response. I struggled with the trauma of emotional life experiences, and I was so used to being there for everyone else that I had failed miserably at being there for myself. It was time to peel back the onion and deal with the ugly truths in my life.

The truth was I left an unhealthy marriage and fell in love with a man who was ready to do life with me. I just didn't know how to handle it. There was nothing my current husband could do to make things better. It was all internal work that I had to do for myself. Imagine feeling like in order to survive you must fight, even when you know you're no longer in danger. I believed in order to get what I needed and wanted that I needed to fight for it.

Growing up, I watched my mother fight all her life. As an adult, I can identify that she handled conflicts from an assertive space. She was stern. She set boundaries, but she was loving all at the same time. My current husband experienced quite the opposite from me. My responses were more of a defense mechanism that I used to protect me from feeling unsafe, any kind of discomfort, and vulnerable even though I had no reason to feel that way. Through my own therapy, I learned our body has a natural response to protect us when we are in danger and because of past traumatic life experiences, my body would send a false signal that caused me to respond with defense even when I was not in harm's way.

I started journaling about my dreams and why they were important to me. I wrote about what I wanted to accomplish: a happy marriage, successful business(es), certain money goals, good health, and the freedom to live without guilt, worry, or shame. I was finally free to be my authentic self, flaws and all. I realized my biggest catalyst was my ability to love myself unconditionally because it freed me to love my life and the people in it unconditionally.

Next, I journaled about what were some of the things that stopped me from reaching my goals, like my thoughts. I also focused on my truths, the most important, of course, was my husband, who is still caring and consistent. He has been rocking by my side for years and has weathered many storms, but none has sent him away. Here I was constantly fighting a fight alone when my husband had been consistent in showing up in love for me. Instead of him hating me for all that I did, he prayed for me. The more I rejected his love, the harder he loved me. At some point, I stopped questioning why he loved me and asked why not. Why did I feel I wasn't worthy to be loved? I mean, if you asked me if I loved myself, I would say, "Hell yeah!" There was no hiding the fact that I was failing in love and in business. I had a man that was riding for me but I wouldn't let him. My actions were not in alignment with my dreams.

The real work began. I had to learn how to trust. I realized I could not have a successful marriage or business without trust. I had to learn to stop and question whether my responses were reactive and coming from a place of protection when there were no threats of danger. Once I became self-aware and intentionally worked on my thoughts and beliefs, my relationship with my husband changed, and it made a difference with our approach to business. This time around, our quest for a new business venture felt different. We no longer argued about location and office furniture. We even came up with the business name together. I no longer felt like I needed to make all the decisions or as if I needed to mark my territory. I was able to enter the business in partnership and operate it as an extension of our love. I could tell that my husband was operating with some caution. He did not want to ruffle any feathers. So, there were some things he would shy away from doing almost as if he was working out of uncertainty. Eventually, he found his lane.

The business has allowed us to do so much more than anticipated. Originally, we opened a private mental health practice with hopes to expand to a group practice. Since our opening, we have expanded to a group practice and opened two additional business entities: a children's outpatient psychiatric clinic and a therapist coaching and consulting business.

After 18-½ years of togetherness, we realize we are just getting started with love, business, and marriage. I guess that's why they say, "Marriage is not for the faint at heart." Although there are many lessons I have learned along the way, one of the biggest takeaways that I can give anyone is to start with you. Before you can build healthy relationships, with others, first you must start with yourself. The moment you feel you have no work to be done is the moment you should seek guidance. Often, we can't see what others see in us. When we work out of survival mode, our actions dictate our outcomes which almost always work against our goals. When all else fails, always go back to your why and reset. This brings me back full circle to my mother, my role model, who taught me the most essential qualities in life and that was the love of God and the value of family. God has been at the center in every aspect of our lives.

It's so amazing to have someone come into your life and expect nothing but the exchange of love. It is through love that you can have peace and harmony. As you can see, getting to this place has not been easy, but it was worth fighting for. Our love, businesses, and marriage is thriving. You can have it all, or, I believe you can have it all. We may have been delayed but we would not be denied.

REFLECTIONS

REFLECTIONS

STANDING FIRM IN MY MANHOOD AND GETTING OUT OF MY OWN WAY

Kyle McDougald

STANDING FIRM IN MY MANHOOD AND GETTING OUT OF MY OWN WAY

Kyle McDougald

Proverbs 18:22, He who finds a wife finds a good thing, and obtains favor from the LORD. (New King James Version)

I was born and raised in a nuclear household with both parents and I am the third of four children. My sister and I are twins, and I am 6 minutes older than she is. I watched my parents work hard to support us, but most importantly, they worked in unity. They had different interests but were willing to show up in support of one other. I watched my mom support my dad as a road captain of the Soul Seekers biker club. In return, dad supported my mom by attending church service on Sunday, which was also dedicated as a family day. We did things as a whole such as taking long rides, going to amusement parks and beaches, or enjoying game night.

When there were disagreements amongst us, we called my grandmother who mediated and deescalated the situation. Dad worked first shift and Mom worked second shift, so they would alternate taking care of us. Although my parents divorced when I was in high school, looking back at my upbringing, I would say my parents' commitment to each other left an impression on what family means to my siblings and me. For example, my two older siblings fell in love and got married as young adults. They have sustained their marriages for 30+ years.

After high school, I attended Central Connecticut State University for two years, but I found myself hanging out in the streets, living the fast life. My mother feared I would get caught up with the wrong crowd, so she sent me to live with my sister in Florida. Changing my environment was a temporary fix. Mentally, I still had the desire to be in the streets, so it was easy to find refuge in Florida. I found lots of girls, drugs, and, eventually, prison. Same thing, different state. Deep down, though, I wanted more.

As I went through life, I didn't know I was trying to fill the void of not having a family that I could call my own. I had two boys by different women and wasn't in a serious relationship with either one. My oldest son lived out of state, and though my younger son was closer, his mom and I had what you might call a strained relationship. I thought I was comfortable just being single, coming and going as I pleased and not really having to focus on responsibilities. I wasn't searching for love at all, at least that's what I told myself. I spent time with women but not in relationships. Let me explain: I was only interested in the pleasure principle and putting on a front for the sake of what I thought was manhood. I didn't care if a woman had children or not. Heck, I played the role of step-parent to several children throughout my lifetime. I have no regrets, but something always seemed to be missing. I failed at making things work, and I stopped trying to fit a square peg in a round hole and trained myself to believe I didn't need family. I was at the darkest place in my life. So, I jeopardized my relationships with my own biological children.

This all changed almost immediately after meeting my wife. There is a saying that you will know love when you see it; you know the person who is the one. I never paid attention to it, but that's what happened when I met my wife. There was something about her that made me want to settle down. She knew what she wanted in life. Tangie came with principles, and she did not play when it came to her family. I remember her asking about my children and telling me how she cannot be in a relationship with someone who didn't have a relationship with their own children. I had to respect that. Through the years and many entanglements, no one thought to ask about my children let alone make it a contingency to deal with me. But she did. She included them on family vacations and offered solutions for disagreements amongst us. She was the glue, and I respected that she cared enough. I had to level up, and not just for her but for me. She was my reminder of the importance of family and how much I yearned to have a family like I did growing up. I was honest with myself and admitted that I wanted a lifetime partner. We began to do things that I hadn't done with anyone else before. We talked about life goals and even planned how we would achieve them. She had children, too, and was coming from a failed marriage. I could feel the pain that she had been through, and I did not want to cause her any more hurt. So, I knew I had to step up my game and be a better protector and provider to my own children.

There is no doubt about it: our love is undeniable. So, when we went through rough patches it was always easy for me to forgive and move on, much easier for me than for her. When we met, the ink was barely dry on her divorce papers, and she carried some reservations about getting together. Trusting and falling in love again was not on her radar. She was rebuilding her family and trying to balance her life in a new normal while I was trying to change my life by gaining full-time employment and building a better relationship with my children. We were a perfect mess and this scared her. Sometimes I felt as if I was all alone, but I could hear God telling me to hold on. He said Tangie was going through her own life battles that had nothing to do with me, and I was called to stand still and be a supportive soldier. I prayed and fasted for her healing as she seemed to resist anything that was of any good to her. I'm not sure when her breakthrough occurred but one day it just happened. The energy in the room felt different. It felt as if the skies opened and she ascended down from the clouds like an angel. The barriers that stood in the way of our relationship were lifted. She was ready to move forward in life. I would say the biggest commonality was our faith in God, wanting to be successful in business, and strengthening our family ties.

All of this was going on in our love life while trying to build a successful business. When it came to establishing financial stability, we had the same vision of business ownership. So, we took the risk and tried several different business ventures; we had a clothing store, a convenience store, a maintenance service, and a plowing company all which were short lived. We were determined to get it right, so we took a closer look at why these businesses were failing.

Our reality was that we had two different views on what running a business entailed. I come from an era where working hard labor meant you were a better provider. Being a boss for me meant being a great hustler, working early mornings and late nights, doing odd jobs, and being busy (which I know doesn't necessarily mean productive). Also, because of my background, I just handled life differently. I grew up in Hartford, CT, a small town where everyone knows each other. And even though I was raised with both parents for most of my childhood, I was not far from the fast life. I lived in the midst of it all. I had friends from all neck of the woods, so hanging out in different places taught me a lot at a young age. I participated in activities that ran counter to my upbringing, but I never forgot where I came from. I was use to transactions that often came from using a barter system or just being a "good dude," looking out for my people in the neighborhood which often did not equate into financial gain. My wife, on the other hand, had a different mindset, and her definition of being a boss meant we needed to work smarter and not harder, building networks and clients from more than inside of our community. Being successful meant developing new business connections with people that we generally would not encounter on a regular basis. This meant, no more hookups just because you're my homie. Budgets, spreadsheets, and tracking profits was how she handled business. This was a hard change for me and often it ended in failed discussions and speechless nights, which caused a strain on our relationship and continued failures in business.

I knew we could not go on this way. I had to get it right and deal with my own belief system. I had to recognize that being a man isn't defined by the type of work I do. Being a man meant living in my truth and holding myself accountable for where I fall short. Being a man meant showing up and taking a stand for all that I believe in. Being a man meant I had to make better efforts in securing a relationship with my children. I had to stop feeling shame about my past behaviors. Being a man meant forgiving myself and letting go. I had to let go of what the streets taught me about being a man. I had to assess what I learned from my own dad who was a skilled laborer who believed in playing as hard as he worked. I had to give myself permission to write my own life story without worrying about the judgment of others.

I prayed that if God gave me a family that I would do right by them. I was prepared and ready for change. This meant walking by faith and taking chances in life. In doing so, I finally felt like I was making a mark in this world and adding meaning in my life. Afraid of old myths but feeling that love was worth the risk. I was all in. I focused on getting my life in order and eventually my children came around more frequently. I was able to take trips to see my older son in Florida for several weeks at a time, and he came to spend time with me as well. I finally felt complete by being able to communicate and spend time with my children.

Tangie also accepted my hand in marriage a decade after she accepted we were meant to be together. This just solidified our relationship on a higher level. We were together for 10 years before we exchanged wedding vows. Some would say, why did it take so long, especially since I asked for her hand in marriage from the beginning of our relationship. But I say it was all in God's timing. I believe if we would have wedded sooner, it probably would not have lasted this long. Our timing was perfect because we were on God's time. Tangie had the time she needed to heal and so did I. For the first time in my life, I was able to focus on my relationship with God. I spent this time getting my soul right. Once I was right spiritually, it seemed like everything else fell into place. We were ready to start a new business venture, my wife's private practice. I would be remiss to say there was not a sign of nervousness. We were at such a good place in our marriage, I did not want to ruffle any feathers. Those negative thoughts of speechless nights and arguments during our prior business encounters definitely came and went, but this time I felt different. I felt ready. I felt solid on who I was and what position I played in my wife's life and in business.

My support was different. I knew that this new business venture had to work or it would cost our relationship. So I decided to work within my own lane. This meant she handled the things that she was good at, and I supported her with the things that I knew how to do best. Compromising in our roles did not seem so bad, but I must admit that it was different. Asking my wife's hand in marriage meant for better or for worse, and although there were times where I felt we were at our worst, I have been able to pull my strength from God.

One of the biggest influences I had in my life was Uncle John who was 91 and lived in Harlem, NY, when he passed away. I would take trips to see him. I spent lots of weekends gaining wisdom when he told stories of his upbringing and relationships. One of the things that helped change my perspective of what a man should be was the way he believed a woman should be treated. Treating a woman well and listening to her heart did not emasculate me, it actually made me better. He reminded me that I had a good woman. So, it was easier for me to loosen my stance in trying to take control or having the final say-so in everything. It made me a better man by accepting who she was as an individual. I stood in my truth in loving her unconditionally, and I took a lot of backlash from others who would say things like, "'Bruh, you your own man. You should be coming and going as you please," or "Ain't no way I'm gone let a woman dictate how I do things." I'll admit, I struggled with listening to my boys versus listening to my lady, but I had to tune all that out and listen to my heart and my God. I'm just thankful that I was obedient, because my friends were all single and none of them were in committed relationships. So, taking their advice on how to manage my relationship would be meaningless since they lacked the knowledge needed to sustain one. Needless to say, back then they would laugh or get mad when I would not show up or partake in activities that were idealized by living as a single man. I was over it, but to them, I was a sucker for love. Today, they know better and respect and understand why I fell in love.

My wife and I sacrificed a lot when it came to our family, like working overnights in inclement weather and putting my health at risk, although our children did not see it at the time. It was important to Tangie and me to show them how to be productive citizens. We prayed they would see our example and that we instilled some of our work ethic into their future.

Looking back at all my life experiences, I can reflect and say that my life turned around when I stopped running from who I was and who people thought I should be. I started to subscribe to who I wanted to become. Being a man meant being faithful in my relationships, starting with myself.

Today, I try to remain positive by reminding myself that I am worthy of all things. I stopped comparing my life to the images and memories of what I saw family life was like. I started creating my own value and belief system and setting my own traditions. I have been able to sustain great relationships with my family while supporting our business.

I contribute to the success in our business by getting out of my own way. I had to let go of the ego that really crippled my relationships with people that were important to me and hold myself accountable for my life choices. If I can lend any advice to couples who are just trying to strive in love, business, and their marriage, it would be to keep God in the midst of all situations. This will result in a rewarding end no matter how dim it may look at times. When faced with adversities go back to your WHY to help you refuel and stay the course.

One of the best things Tangie and I have incorporated throughout our relationship is time spent together. We enjoy long rides along the East Coast but we also enjoy flying to different countries and exploring life. When we can't get away, we find opportunities to do things locally. Yes, date nights still exist. We enjoy going to the beach, going on walks or taking long rides on my motorcycle. My point is to find time to enjoy things of interest and use those things to help you get back to the reason why you fell in love. Having love, business, and marriage can work if you're willing to both put in the work.

Today we are at a happy balance where our business has been able to flourish. We have expanded our private practice to a group practice. We also opened another business entity that provides psychotherapy services to children. Just to think we went from struggling to manage our relationship and past business ventures to managing our love relationship while running a business with 15 employees and growing. Love, business and marriage requires work. Both parties in the relationship have to be willing, accountable, and committed to put in the necessary work. To God Be The Glory.

REFLECTIONS

REFLECTIONS

#TEAM WOFFORD

WHEN THE HONEYMOON IS OVER, STICK AND STAY!

Lashonda Wofford

WHEN THE HONEYMOON IS OVER, STICK AND STAY!

Lashonda Wofford

Marriage is not an institution for pooling money and skills together. It's a place where two people unite to achieve God's highest purpose. -Ngina Otiende

Love: Google defines love as an intense feeling of deep affection or a great interest and pleasure in something.

Marriage: Google also tells us that marriage is the legally or formally recognized union of two people as partners in a personal relationship.

I define love and marriage as a roller coaster ride with the person you want to spend the rest of your natural life with. This lifelong roller coaster ride has bumps, big and small, and there are a lot of ups and downs, hurdles low and high, twists and turns, sunny days and other days when it's pouring. These things are extremely hard to navigate, but navigating through them with the right partner makes it easier. The old saying, "You will do anything for the person you love," is factual. Love is a beautiful bond between two people that takes a lot of time and even more work to make strong. Love is unconditional and it is giving willingly without stipulations or unrealistic expectations. Often, we think we know what love really is based on what we may see or have seen. We think marriage is easy based on the way others portray it. When two people decide to become one they must also decide what their love story will be; they have to decide as a couple what works for them and what doesn't.

When I met my husband, Travis, 15 years ago, it was not love at first sight. Did I think he was attractive? Absolutely, but I was not looking for love, and I know for sure he was not looking for love either. The interesting thing is that we met through my sister and her ex-husband.

To celebrate my sister's birthday one year, she invited me to go out with her, her (now ex) husband, and a few of her friends. I was never really big on clubbing or the nightlife, but it was for her birthday, and she knew I wasn't going to say no.

Needless to say, I did go and that was the first time I actually saw and had a conversation with my husband. My first thoughts of him included, "Oh, Lord, he's one of them," and that he would just hang on the wall and talk to every woman in the room, so I was far from interested. When we finally made it to the club, the line was really long and I remember thinking that people really stand in line for this. As we waited to get into the club, I saw Travis walk to the front of the line and start a conversation with one of the bouncers at the door. The next thing I know, he told us to come to the front of the line. The wait was over. Okay, he had some pull, and I was low key impressed. Finally, we made it inside the club and it was not what it was cracked up to be. It felt like it was 1,000 degrees inside the building, the smell of sweat, musk and booty filled the air, and I was ready to exit stage left. I didn't care how much it cost to get in, I was done, and everybody knew it. Then, just as we were getting ready to leave, Travis noticed a staircase and another door so he suggested that we see what was going on upstairs. Reluctantly, I went with the group, and low and behold, there was cold air conditioning with no smell. It was like two different buildings. I could not understand why anyone would prefer to be downstairs in all that when this space was right upstairs, but anyway.

We found a nice section to sit down. The music was nice, and the vibe was great. We were having fun. Everybody hit the dance floor except me; I was watching, just chilling and relaxing. Travis stood beside me and we talked a little bit. The DJ played a song that I really liked, and I wanted to dance, but I didn't want to lose my seat, so I turned to Travis and said, " Can you hold my seat? I want to go dance." He said, "No."

I was shocked but okay. Then he said, "No, because how do you know that I don't want to dance, too?"

"Oh, okay. My bad. I didn't think you wanted to dance," I told him.
So we headed to the dance floor and had a ball. We actually danced the entire night away. We laughed, danced, and talked for the rest of the night. There was chemistry, and neither of us could deny it. After the club, we went out to eat, and I am not sure how, but Travis ended up riding back in the car with me, my sister, and her (now ex) husband. Travis and I were in the back seat, laughing and talking as he laid his head on my lap.

The night came to an end. There was something about him; his perfect chocolate skin, his bright smile, his gentleness, his personality, or the mixture of it all, he stayed on my mind. I had never met a man like him before. We stayed in touch, and when the timing was right, we connected. I remember a conversation we had, and he mentioned that he doesn't understand why everyone feels like the man has to be the one to buy flowers, do nice things for the woman, wine and dine her. He asked why it is not okay for a woman to propose to a man if she really loves him. I knew then that I had to show him affection, appreciation, and wine and dine him sometimes, too. As things became more serious between us, the time was right, so I proposed to him. Yep, I did, because I wanted him to know how important he was to me and that I wasn't too prideful to ask him for his hand in marriage. Of course, he was shocked that I remembered the conversation and that I asked, but he said yes. We spent 2008 planning our wedding. In September 2009, we did it. We tied the knot and the day was so perfect.

When the wedding and the honeymoon were over, life started happening. I was never one to budget and didn't always make smart decisions with my money. I was used to calling my own shots and doing what I pleased. My husband was the total opposite. He always budgeted, spent money wisely, made smart money moves, and made strategic decisions that would prove beneficial now and later. I came from a strong line of independent Black women who taught us to never let a man tell us what to do, to do what we wanted to do, and to make our own money. Combined with the control issues from a previous relationship, I was a financial disaster. This was not good, and we had so many arguments that appeared to be about finances, but in actuality, were caused by my past.

One day, we were in yet another heated argument, and I was reaching shutdown mode. Travis looked at me with tears in his eyes and said, "Baby, I am not your enemy. I love you, and I got married to stay married. I am not trying to control you or tell you what to do but I have to look out for our future. I am not that guy that hurt you by trying to control your every move and telling you what to do with money. I am also not that guy with bottomless pockets. I am not David (my first husband) or Mr. George (my daddy), and I am trying, but you have to help me, too."

In that moment, my heart was crushed just seeing how much pain I had caused my husband. I apologized to him, and I meant every word of my apology, but here comes the hard part: the work. In that moment, I realized there were things I carried over from previous relationships, and I had to let all that go. Before I proposed to Travis, God told me how He sent me someone, and we would love, evolve, and build together. My husband was and is my gift from God. I promised God that I would always cherish, protect, and respect him. I realized that it was time for me to fight for my marriage. I was the problem, and I had to change my ways before I lost him.

My fear of losing my husband was greater than any other fear I'd had in a very long time. My prayers changed, becoming more strategic as I asked God for guidance and to change my mindset. I needed God to help me unlearn everything I had been taught or had heard, indirectly or directly, about marriage. The more I prayed the more God spoke to me and turned those unhealthy behaviors around. My husband and I understood that we only had each other; we are the team. It will always be us against the world, so we must be strong as a unit. We incorporated rules for our finances: (1) purchases over $500 would be discussed and only done if there was mutual agreement; (2) money that went into our savings account (from both of us) couldn't be touched; and (3) budgeting for paying bills, to name a few. This worked much better. As circumstances changed, we learned to quickly pivot to survive. As I continued the inner work on healing from my past and changing my thought process, things between Travis and I got better and better. I saw the weight being lifted off my husband's shoulders. I never wanted, nor do I want to contribute any kind of added stress to Travis' plate. I want to always be his peace.

I must admit we had a time with finances. It took years of hard work and dedication from both of us to make it work. More than anything, it took a lot of patience, and my husband had to extend so much grace to me. I am sure there were a few times he was almost ready to throw in the towel, but thank God we made it through. Just as it seemed like we were finally on track with finances, the next test arrived.

I laugh at this now, because Lord knows, we could not have survived both tests at the same time. Six months after we were married—it was a Wednesday—I came home from a very long day of work. Travis asked to talk to me in the living room. This made me nervous. He told me a little boy he had pretty much raised as his nephew, even though they were not related by blood, needed to stay with us for a few months. The boy's mother (whom my husband had known and referred to as a "cousin") needed time to get on her feet, to find another job and a stable place to stay. Did I know this lady? No, but what I did know was Kristopher was only six, and I would never turn a child away that needed help. So, I said sure, he can come. We had an extra bedroom already fixed up that no one ever slept in, so it was fine. Kristopher was due to arrive on Saturday. We only had a few days to prepare and needed a family meeting to talk to our daughter, ShaQuandra, who was 12 years old. Travis explained the situation to her and she answered, "Well, I know y'all are going to let him come, right? If he's only six, he has to have somewhere to stay. Perfect!"

On Saturday, Kristopher's mother dropped him off. Oh my goodness, he was so small and so cute. We showed him around the house and the kids' area where they had their own living room, bathroom, and bedrooms. We showed Kristopher his room, and his eyes and face lit up with excitement. He could not believe that he had his own room and his own bed. He told us that he had never had his own room or his own bed before. Wow, I thought. He is six and has never had his own room or his own bed. I was glad we could be there for him. I knew we had to give him the ultimate childhood experience while he was with us.

As we were going through his things, hanging his clothes in the closet, and folding them to put away in the dresser, I realized Kristopher didn't have any good clothes. All his pants were too short or too small. He didn't have any long sleeve shirts, jackets or coats, underwear, socks, or anything that fit. I was registering him for school on Monday morning, so he needed clothes and shoes. I continued going through the clothes, and when I got to the bottom of the last bag, I saw his legal documents: his social security card, original birth certificate, and a handwritten note signed and dated by his mom giving me and Travis the rights and permission to make all decisions regarding her son.

I got scared because I had no idea what we just signed up for. Needing to buy Kristopher clothes, and making him comfortable for a while was one thing. Not knowing if his mother was ever coming back to get him was a whole different ball game. Everything in me was telling me she wasn't coming back to get him, but I ignored the previous red flag of how this woman didn't know me and didn't care to meet me or have a conversation with me before just dropping her kid off with us. But this one I couldn't ignore. I took the documents and the handwritten letter to our bedroom and showed them to Travis and told him I didn't think she had any plans to come back to get Kristopher. Travis disagreed and thought I was just overreacting and reading too much into the documents and the letter.

We went shopping that day as planned to get what Kristopher needed, and he was so excited and appreciative. I focused on how to make him feel welcome and a part of our family. Later, I would find out that no matter how much we tried to include him and love him, the void from his mom could never be filled.

Months went by, then years, and Kristopher's mom never came

back to get him. One of the things that bothered me the most was how it seemed she was living her best life while we were raising and supporting her child. She provided no support; not financial, physical, moral, emotional. Nothing. Kristopher learned how to manipulate at an early age, and he played Travis and I against each other. It took Travis longer to see it, but once he did, we put our son in counseling because he needed more than we could give him in certain areas. Kristopher dealt with abandonment and trust issues plus mental health challenges passed down to him through his birth family. Even though I knew and understood all of this, raising him was still challenging. There were so many days during my drive home from work that I just dreaded walking in the door. I contemplated leaving my husband so many times because it felt like love wasn't enough. I thought about how I didn't sign up for any of it.

My anger with Kristopher's mother grew to the point where I started internalizing my feelings. My frustration led to outbursts with my family that I had to later apologize for saying things I did not mean. I remembered that Kristopher was just a little boy, and none of it was his fault. Once I put her and what she wasn't doing out of my mind, it was easier to focus on him, our family and what we could do to help him become the best person he could be despite his mom not being in his life.

Shifting my focus to provide for and raise our children did help for a while. Then I learned that before he was born, Kristopher's mother had two daughters and gave them up to a woman in North Carolina. They were raised together. As for Kristopher, his mother left him more than once. The first time was when he was just nine months old. She dropped him off with Travis's mother and picked him up when he was two. She held onto him until she dropped him off with us. So, my initial thoughts and feelings were right. I should have never ignored the red flags, especially because Travis knew about all of it.

I became angry with my husband because I felt like all of this should have been disclosed at the time he asked me if Kristopher could stay with us for a couple of months. I didn't have all the details, and when I showed him all the legal documents with the handwritten note giving us rights, that should have rung a bell and prompted him to tell me about her history as an absent mom. I don't think that would have changed my decision, but it would've been clearer to me that this was not going to be short term at all. I would've prepared for this journey a little bit differently.

It took a while, a lot of conversations and even more prayer, but eventually, we both understood that we were on an assignment and it was not about us. God had given us this responsibility because He trusted us and He knew we could be trusted with such a task. We shifted our focus to being and operating as a team so that we could give Kris what he needed.

Since then, we showed both ShaQuandra and Kristopher to keep God in the front, middle, and end of everything they do and that marriage is beautiful. Marriage requires constant nurturing and lots of compromising from both parties without sacrificing love. We have taught them that true love will always win. Both ShaQuandra and Kristopher have told us that we inspired them and watching us has helped them see that anything is possible. There is no dream that is not obtainable if you believe and put in the time. It wasn't easy but it's been worth it all. Looking back, important lessons I've learned about love and marriage are as follows:

• Heal from your past before you decide to get married. It's unfair to your spouse to pay for and suffer because of your unhealed past;

• Wives, it is just as much our responsibility to make our husbands feel loved, appreciated, valued, wanted, and special as it is theirs to do the same for us;

• Make sure you take the time to really SEE your spouse for who he or she is;

• Trust your husband to LEAD as he is being LED by God. No matter what, make time for each other;

• Cover your spouse, cover your household, and cover your business in daily prayer.

REFLECTIONS

REFLECTIONS

SACRIFICES YOU MAKE FOR LOVE

Travis Wofford

SACRIFICES YOU MAKE FOR LOVE

Travis Wofford

If you want to grow as a couple or individual. You have to get comfortable with being uncomfortable.

How do we know what love looks like? Who do we learn it from? Most people learn from their parents or other couples they see growing up. For many people, they're unsure. Depending on who you ask, you can get many different answers. For me, it's being affectionate, attentive, flirtatious, supportive, compassionate, good communicator and being willing to make sacrifices for the ones you love. I also feel being a protector, a provider, a supportive friend, and a faithful lover are important. However, it also depends on the needs of your spouse. I learned people change over time, so when they change, their needs change as well. No one ever told me any of this; I had to learn these things as I got older.

How can you know who to love? This is definitely a hard one to answer. Most people don't want to put themselves out there if the feelings aren't mutual, but you can't know if it's mutual if you don't put yourself out there. I tried it a couple of times; sometimes I hurt people, and sometimes I got hurt. Those experiences turned me away from trying to find someone to love.

Years before we officially met, I remember seeing Lashonda (everyone calls her Shon) around the way. She hung out with my cousin in the neighborhood where I grew up. I knew everyone around there except Shon. I remember she might have been 4'8", weighed 90 pounds, and she was pregnant. I remember asking who got that little girl pregnant because they were going to jail. I didn't think she was even a teenager, but they told me she was older. Four years later, I lived outside the city, and I saw her driving around. I learned Shon lived on the same road I did. We never interacted, just passed each other, and I always noticed she had a little girl with her. As time went on, I saw less of them, so I figured they had moved. Word on the streets was that she had gotten married, and that her husband was paralyzed as a result of being shot. I remember thinking I hate that for all of them. After that, I didn't hear much more about them. Time went on and I was invited to my homeboy's wedding reception. As it turns out, he married Shon's sister. At the reception, I saw Shon and her daughter come in. They were both wearing white and looked really nice. What really caught my attention was the ray of sunlight behind them, shining on their heads. I'm not sure if anyone else saw it or if that was only meant for me to notice as some kind of sign of what was to come many years later.

On the night I met my wife, I wasn't looking for love. As a matter of fact, I wasn't looking for anything at all. I had a situation that I was trying to get out of, and that was my focus. I was also trying to find my place in the world. I had been promoting parties and clubs to some success but I hadn't gotten over the hump into making real money yet. The night we went out for her sister's birthday I really invited myself. My friend, who was her sister's then-husband, was cutting my hair, and they were talking over my head about their plans to go out for her birthday.

"So no one's going to invite me?" I asked. I was really joking, but they told me to come. When we met to go out, my friend and I were the only two men with about six women. It was cool because I knew everyone really well but Shon. At this point in my life, I knew a lot of people in a lot of different places, so I had some ideas about where to go. I called people in the city we were in asking where to go and they gave us some spots to check out. We got to the spot, and the line was super long. No one wanted to wait, so I paid for us to skip the line. Once inside, the club was packed and hot but the second floor was nicer. Shon's sister told me to take Shon to the floor and dance, but I was trying to peep the scene and check the group for a minute. That's when Shon asked me to hold her seat while she went and danced. I looked and asked how she knew I wasn't going to dance? She looked so surprised, and we ended up dancing together the whole night.

There were a lot of sparks between us, and we really enjoyed each other at the club. I ended up riding home in the same car, and the sparks were still there. While we talked, I got the surprise of my life; she told me she could sing. I heard back in the day she could sing but never heard it for myself, so I asked her to sing something. She opened her mouth, and if I wasn't in the car to witness it myself, I would not have believed it was her. I was shocked and amazed at how such a big voice could come out of someone so small. Even though there were sparks, the timing wasn't right for either of us so that was it for the time being.

Not long after our night out, I got out of my situation. I was single and enjoying myself. I had my own place with a roommate that was hardly ever home so most of the time it was just me. For most of my adult life, my mom had been sickly and I stayed at home until my late 20's. I was finally on my own, and for the first time in my life, I was putting myself first. I always made sure my momma and younger sister had what they needed, but I needed to figure out what I liked and how I wanted to live. I knew how to pay bills because I had been doing that since I was 18, but I wanted to know I could really take care of myself. Even though I moved out, I still helped my momma with certain bills because she was on a fixed income, and my sister had recently had my niece.

I worked 12-hour nights, so I only worked 15 to 18 days a month. I still was promoting clubs and into the nightlife. I wasn't in that venture alone; I had two partners to help with the load. Even with the three of us, it was hectic. We definitely didn't have banker hours. A lot of times, I wouldn't get home from promoting until 2 or 3 a.m., which was cool because I was single. There wasn't anyone at home waiting for me. Being a promoter at that time, you had to be in the streets. If you wanted people to support your event, you had to support theirs. Also, there were a lot of females that would notice you and try to get close to what they thought you had. I can't say I didn't indulge. I was single and wasn't looking for any type of commitment. I also let it be known that I wasn't looking for anything serious. I was seeing a couple of different women at this time. I was always honest; I let them know I was seeing other people.

I wasn't interested in anything serious, but for whatever reason, some felt they could make me change my mind. Well, to be honest, one finally did. It was Shon because she wasn't being pushy or demanding about it. She was my friend, made me laugh and checked on me from time to time. That meant more to me than anything. Shon and I started communicating more regularly after keeping in touch here and there after the night of her sister's birthday. We ended up getting closer than I expected sooner than I expected. We talked on the phone for hours and we started going out. She was working a lot, and so was I, but we made time for each other. One day, we were at my house. I was in the living room watching TV when Shon called me into the bedroom. When I walked in, she was holding an earring, and I asked if she needed help finding the other one.

"This isn't mine," she said.

"Okay, then throw it away," I answered before heading back to the living room to watch TV.

She sat down beside me and asked if we could talk. She understood that I wasn't looking for anything serious, but she didn't like the idea of other women being around me in my house, my room, or my bed. At that moment, I knew I had to make a choice. She didn't ask me to, but when she told me how she felt, I knew what had to be done. I told her I was trying to get myself together. I really wanted to work on myself, and that I did care for her, so I was willing to give us a chance. Not too long after that, my roommate moved out, and Shon and her daughter, ShaQuandra, moved in.

Shon is the first woman I lived with other than relatives, so I had no idea what to expect. It was definitely life changing for me. I was still promoting clubs at this time. Shon knew I enjoyed promoting and the night life, but she was the total opposite. She was an early bird and I was a night owl. Also, I was very social and she didn't like being around large crowds of people. This sometimes caused friction between us. I was use to coming and going as I pleased and not answering questions about where I was going, when I was coming back, who I was with, etc. And please don't let the plans change and I didn't mention it! That was not good. For example, if me and my friends went out and started at one bar but ended up at another spot without Shon knowing, she felt as if I was being deceitful. I quickly realized she had trust issues with men. I know I had a past, but I hadn't done anything to make her not trust me. If she woke up at a certain time, and I wasn't home, she would blow my phone up. I also realized the issue was deeper than just lack of trust. Shon actually had anxiety if I didn't answer because of what happened to her first husband. I did my best to make her feel secure and at ease. It was just something that was going to take some time. Eventually, I started to lose my interest in promoting. Some of it had to do with Shon and some didn't. I guess that season in my life was over, and I had to find something else.

Shortly after moving in together, we got engaged, which was crazy because Shon actually proposed to me. She had a ring and all. I said yes, but I was still kind of tripping off of being proposed to and being someone's husband. I didn't know too many happily married couples. I had no idea what it really meant to be a husband and a father, too. Just a couple of months earlier, I was a bachelor. I had to figure this out quickly and I had to get it right.

After we married, we realized the honeymoon was over and we were back to the real world. A few months later, my cousin said she was going through some things and needed help getting back on her feet. She asked if we could take her son, Kristopher, and since I had been his father figure, I told her I would talk to Shon about it and let her know. My cousin had two previous children she had given up already so I didn't want that to happen to him. Shon and I discussed it and we both agreed since this was supposed to be temporary. I knew there was the possibility of it being long-term, and even though Shon doesn't remember me saying that, I'm pretty sure I did because I knew what happened with my cousin's other kids. Kristopher moved in, and at first everything was okay, but Shon and I had disagreements about things having to do with him. We got no financial support from his mama, and that made me feel some type of way. But I finally accepted that she wasn't going to help or keep the promises she made to him when she called. She would tell him she's coming to get him and sometimes she would, sometimes she wouldn't. We were left with a depressed six-year-old who couldn't figure out what was really going on. I got over his mama a lot quicker than Shon did. Once I focused on Kristopher, then I got over her.

At this point in our lives, I worked two jobs; first shift Monday through Friday and a part-time position from 5 to 9 p.m. three nights a week. I also worked half days every other Saturday. My time was limited, and there wasn't enough of me to go around. Shon and I were newlyweds who never got to really enjoy each other. Our son had issues with abandonment and wanted my attention. Our daughter was the only one who didn't really ask for my time because she was still trying to figure me out. I wanted to spend time with both of them and have time with my wife. Shon and I argued all the time, and it got to the point. I didn't think we would make it. Kristopher was not my son by birth, but I was the only father he'd known. I could also relate to him because at points during my teen years, I had not always lived with my mama. I knew how it felt to have somewhere to stay that doesn't feel like home. I knew how it felt to try to stay out of the way so you wouldn't make anyone mad and get told to leave. I knew how it felt to be a child caught in the middle of adult problems. I wasn't going to allow Kristopher to go through that, and I was afraid it was going to cost me my marriage.

Time went on, and we continued to have issues with our son and his mother, but that wasn't our biggest hurdle. Like most couples, finances remained a stressor. No matter how much I tried to work with Shon, she had her own ways when it came to money. All I wanted was stability, security, and a nest egg. Shon began to want more out of life, and I had no problem with her wanting to do better, but I did have a problem with taking from the house to do other things. Once Shon sets her mind on doing something, she has tunnel vision. All she sees is the target. That's cool if you have the capital to back it, but if not, then you should have a great plan to execute. Patience is just not something she has when she sees something she wants. I never wanted to hold her back on her dreams but we couldn't jeopardize our livelihood for it. I grew up without having a lot, and I didn't want our family to go through that.

There was a point where our finances were so bad, my budget was $3 dollars a day. Working these jobs had me so stressed out. I was sleep deprived and thought I was going to lose my mind. Shon didn't realize that I was going through this. She had her bills to pay and I had mine. I worked my way out of that hole, and I thought everything would be good. I found a job that paid more, so I didn't have to work so much. I felt like everything began to level out. We bought our first house together, our daughter was graduating high school and expecting our grandson, and then Shon said she wanted to quit her job to start our own business.

I was cool with it, but what was the plan? Where was the money coming from? How would we make it without two incomes? I wasn't trying to be negative; I needed us to talk about the answers to these questions. This caused an argument because she felt I wasn't being supportive and that I was content with how things were and with what we had. She also felt I didn't believe in her. Both of those things were not true; I just didn't want our family to be strained and for us to lose all we had worked for.

We needed a plan and a blessing from God. The blessing came when I received a job that doubled my income and allowed Shon to pursue her goal to become a business owner and entrepreneur. The business is flourishing, and I have moved up in my job. The goals have changed, but my family is always my biggest priority. My job keeps me on the road and away from home, but it allows Shon to grow the business that benefits our family unit the same as does my job. Sometimes you have to make sacrifices for the ones you love. Happy Spouse, Happy House!

REFLECTIONS

REFLECTIONS

#TEAM SIMMONS

PAY TO PLAY!

Dr. Sh'nai Simmons

PAY TO PLAY!

Dr. Sh'nai Simmons

Play keeps us vital and alive. Lucia Capachione

As a precocious freshman in college, I was in Buffalo, New York, for a purpose: I was determined to change the trajectory of my addiction-plagued family and hell bent on rescuing my siblings from the New York State foster care system. I enrolled in two programs for a double major in education and psychology with a Spanish minor. I really was not looking for a life partner. I entertained a guy because, heck, it felt good to be desired, but I was just distracting myself from a painful series of unproductive male acquaintances.

One evening, while goofing around at the public pay phone in the dorms, this guy got off the elevator. Now, this was significant because although it was a co-ed dorm, the dorm was primarily female so any guys who did not reside in that dorm were going to stick out, and this guy stuck out for sure. He seemed to be flirting with me and I welcomed it. A freshman getting the attention of an upperclassman was another level. The night ended uneventfully, and I thought nothing of it until the next day when I ran into the same guy as I was walking through the student center. He invited me to walk with him to the Bursar's office and I agreed. I cannot tell you why this dude intrigued me so much. That walk led to a later chat in my dorm and some petting until I remembered I was in a relationship. He kindly let me know that I had options to consider and left me to ponder.

Well, I did not ponder very long. I decided that there was something about this dude that I wanted to have more of and dumped my boyfriend soon after. Once I told 'Ole Flirty—Taiwan—what I decided, the roller coaster ride of our relationship began. It was exhilarating! It seemed that we spent every waking, free moment together. We talked all night long, learning of each other's family woes and trauma-laden backgrounds. I was warned about his history periodically, but it did not matter to me. I was enthralled with this young man and open to tell the truth about it. I remember the night our relationship became public. He had stayed over in my dorm room past curfew, and we had a fire drill in the middle of the night. It was pretty apparent at that point he was with me. We had a very passionate and physical chemistry that would often begin with public play fighting (like slap boxing) and work us into very sensual evenings. Yes, this was all in the dormitories. Eventually, we both ran our roommates away. We tried to hide our relationship to keep things simple and avoid the drama of dating a "player."

As we grew in our friendship and realized we wanted to do life together for the long haul, our lives got more intense. I shared my intent to get my siblings—my 9- and 12-year-old sisters and my 10-year-old brother—out of foster care and explained that I was a package deal. To my surprise, this did not phase him at all. Taiwan shared my value of taking care of family and jumped onboard the journey to convince the Bureau of Child Welfare that we were a good fit for the children. That was a long and uphill battle, but we committed to doing whatever it took.

We had to get married, move into nonresidential housing, and be trained as licensed foster care parents for the state of New York. So, that is exactly what we did, and we did it through job transitions, withdrawing from college, and the loss of our first child. That is a lot to tackle as a newly married couple in their early twenties with no examples of successful marriages to follow. We struggled, and we paid a hefty price for what some may consider to be the admirable goal of getting the children out of foster care.

Taiwan and I were married on December 27, 1996, while hosting the children for their Christmas vacation. When he tells it, he says he was tricked into getting married two days after Christmas so I could have a steady stream of gifts during the season. The truth is that I was pregnant the month before with our first son and was unable to carry him to term. On December 1st of 1996, I had what doctors call a spontaneous miscarriage. We were devastated, but we settled in our spirit that God knew best and maybe it was an opportunity to focus on getting the children out of foster care. We decided to move up our wedding plans and get married by a justice of the peace while the children were with us, so they could be a part of the ceremony. Our friends and family helped us pull off a reception in our home, and it was a done deal. We were husband and wife on a mission. Our son, Christian, was born in April 1998, and two months later, the children were officially placed in our care. Shortly after Christian's first birthday, I learned I was pregnant with our daughter, Cache. She was born in July 2000. Our mission to make a home for my younger siblings was completed in 1999 when we successfully adopted them. The date was even more important because it marked the nine-year anniversary of their foster care placement.

One would think we were now able to breathe since we accomplished what we set out to do. We were now full-time parents doing the best we could to figure that out. Truth be told, we had no clue what we were doing. I was consumed with navigating parenthood and trying desperately to avoid all my mom's mistakes. I was 23 years old, a mom of three children, and one on the way, a full-time supervisor of a human services program and a new convert to the Christian faith. Taiwan and I had dabbled a bit in the multi-level marketing business industry and noted some potential examples of healthy Christian marriages. While I did not know much about being a wife at that time, I knew I was not doing it well.

While on a women's retreat weekend, I really felt the Lord showing me areas where I need to improve; specifically, that my role as a wife was not to attempt to shape my husband. I was recharged and refocused and ready to declare my recommitment and devotion to Taiwan. I called him with excitement one of the nights I was away, but he did not respond with the same energy. I was disappointed, but I figured he was just overwhelmed from being home alone with all the children. I shrugged it off and refocused on the retreat agenda.

Once I got back home and resumed our routine, I was determined to put into practice the things that were downloaded in my heart while away. Taiwan and I were on different work schedules. One day he called me home for my lunch break for a chat. That lunch was earth shattering. The love of my life who had always made me feel safe and supported my every endeavor told me that he had been unfaithful. I could barely catch my breath. I was in so much emotional pain, I was numb. I was also perplexed. Why would God charge me to show up differently in my marriage knowing that my husband had not been faithful to me? I felt trapped. I was in my last trimester of pregnancy with a toddler and two adolescent children. What in the world was I going to do? I really had no clue. I stuffed every thought and feeling that surfaced and went back to work, attempting to act as if my heart was not broken. I failed miserably. It was apparent that I was not well, but I pressed on anyway.

During the following weeks, I focused on preparing for the delivery of my baby girl. I knew enough about prenatal wellness to know it was vitally important for me to be as emotionally stable as possible. It was hard. I had fits of anger and actual rage that alternated with feelings of shame and failure. I needed to shift my thoughts to something positive to not harm my baby. Cache came a little late by way of induced labor, and I absolutely adored her.

At the same time, I was terrified, exhausted, and frustrated. My beautiful bundle of joy was not easy to manage. She had jaundice, thrush, and colic. She seemed to be extending my prenatal stress into my postpartum weeks, and I was over it.

What was I going to do? I leaned heavily on the children's godmother, my good friend, Annetta, for postpartum assistance, but I did so without revealing the breach in my marriage. I just could not bring myself to talk about it. I was living one day at a time, traversing my emotional storm and fears about the future. I was unable to see a path forward as a single mom and opted to stay in my marriage.

It took me a long time to be able to admit that I stayed because I was afraid to face the shame of the truth and challenges as a single mom of four children. I did not want to be seen as a failure.

I did not want to revisit a life of poverty. I did not want to be a statistic. I did not want to figure out how to coparent and share time with my kids. I did not want my children living in two different homes. So, I decided that I would work through the pain and distrust. I decided to get an understanding of how we found ourselves in distress. I also decided I was not going to tolerate anything less than what I deserved. I adapted a righteous indignation and asserted my demands. I demanded complete transparency and accountability at all times moving forward. I demanded space, patience, and tolerance for my emotional outbursts. I demanded growth!

We were in an uphill battle and decided we could benefit from a fresh start, so we moved to Virginia to be closer to Christian couples we previously identified as good examples for us to follow. That relocation reawakened our entrepreneurial goals. The wives in the business that caught my attention were different. They worked well with their spouses, they were included in the business, they had defined roles and a notable level of security. These wives were professionally complementary and intrigued me. I admired them and gleaned from them certain ways to conduct myself.

This shift in my focus helped to assuage the emotional scarring and a pathway for healing was forged. Don't mistake that to mean that there were no more challenges. That was far from the truth. We were still in our early twenties just learning how to be adults, figuring out who we were as individuals, and trying to reinvent the models of parenthood that were left for our reference.

In Virginia, the six of us lived in a two-bedroom apartment for the first few months. Surprisingly, it was the most peaceful time I had experienced in my adult life. As we settled into our new state and secured employment, we also focused on defining our joint goals. First, it was buying our first home. Then it was growing our careers. What we found was that as we learned to work together, the healing progressed. We were growing stronger and stronger as a unit. Team Simmons was underway, and our confidence was strengthening in one another. We worked on our communication and on creating safety for the other to be honest and forthright so no secrets could live between us.

Taiwan grew in his ability to set boundaries, which was an absolute necessity in his career as an insurance agent. We soon learned that married men in our area were very much desired by single women and Taiwan would need awareness of the "opportunities" that presented themselves. As I matured, I learned to identify that although charisma was needed for Taiwan to be successful in sales it was a slippery slope. So he and I had difficult talks about the way he did his job as an insurance agent and the importance of implementing boundaries.

As our marriage grew stronger, we became intentional about feeding it with healthy examples and practical skills. This concerted effort to grow drew other people to us who had marriage troubles. We felt a sense of obligation to help them as best as we could. To do so with integrity, we knew we had to be whole and became even more impassioned about having a healthy union ourselves. We learned from business partners, by watching other couples with strong marriages, reading books, and listening to tapes. We went to marriage conferences and seminars and always maintained a keen interest in other tenured marriages. After a while, I realized there really was nothing new under the sun. We were devout Christians and all the good tips we learned were simply extracted from the Bible.

We noted some variations in how people interpreted the Word of God and found that some of the precepts were hard to implement. For instance, the idea of not going to bed angry did more harm than good at first. We would attempt to stay up and resolve issues, but I would notoriously fall asleep because nothing gets in the way of my sleep.

This presented a great challenge because Taiwan wanted me to focus on the matter, but I would become irritable and respond in abrasive ways. Sometimes tempers would fly, and we would simply exacerbate the original issue. We eventually found ways to reconcile our idiosyncrasies with what the text said by recognizing that we live by grace and do not have to be subjected to legalism. These experiences and others motivated us to think about how we could help other married couples.

There was no question about it; God was moving us to use our mess to help other couples. We loved the idea but had to tackle the insecurity associated with that process. We saw so much pain in other couples and we totally understood how people could get there. We knew what it felt like to try our hardest and still come up with the same unhelpful results. We had our own experience of feeling let down just days, if not hours, following a marriage enrichment event because although we understood the principles that were taught, we were challenged in successfully executing them. The theory was clear and we agreed with the precepts taught.

We were challenged with identifying the specific strategies as there were little to no opportunities to learn experientially. We understood the principles. Call it creativity or maybe even our ADHD (Taiwan says he does not have it but everyone in our home does!), but we eventually became inspired to engage couples with a hands-on approach. I distinctly remember pulling an all-nighter at one couple's home as we attempted to help them work through their challenges.

Don't ask me, because today I do not remember exactly what we were doing, but I do remember waking up and making breakfast in their kitchen. We left feeling like we had a meaningful impact.

Today, we do things a bit differently, although we are never above a good house call. It is so special to help usher peace into a union under duress. We have been able to marry our spiritual growth and callings with the invaluable experiences of our careers. Taiwan and I both have been graced with the gift to work with people. We have both been trained as ropes and initiative course instructors where the skills essential for effective teamwork is necessary to successfully complete the course. Taiwan continues to serve the community as an associate pastor at our church and insurance agent. I am a licensed professional counselor in Virginia and Florida, where we now reside.

We co-own and lead our mental health group practice where we have acquired additional marriage enrichment skills from expert trainers. The culmination of these experiences and downloads from the Holy Spirit has thrust us into launching our own model of marriage enrichment based on the power of play.

In 2021, we conceived Play-Fuelled Marriages, an initiative of the Get In Touch Network that specifically infuses empirically validated marriage strengthening tools into an interactive game-oriented experience for couples. We customize activities to transcend knowledge of the content often taught in marriage seminars and provoke couples to engage and apply the information. We have the unique ability of injecting both partners with an infectious combination of humorous competition and a desire for healthier interactions.

We love helping couples see their individual and collective strengths and we highlight them during our events so they feel the support and encouragement of other couples. When couples are celebrated in front of other couples, it reinforces their efforts and inspires others to adopt the same practices. Overall, we help couples grow through play.

Twenty-six years of marriage and counting, we are stronger today than ever before. We are thrilled to see this season of our union, to live how we want to live. We paid a hefty price to be here, but we learned so much. I can say I am more in love with Taiwan now than I was when we lived in the dorms. Back then it was all lust, today we walk in time-tested, tenured love. Every day ain't easy but it is all worth it.

I get to do life with my best friend, business partner, baby daddy, lover, and confidante. It just doesn't get any better than this!

The best advice, from my own experience, that I would share with other couples are:

• Build your marriage from a common, larger purpose. For us it was God, His Word, and a desire to destroy generational patterns;

• Keep the lines of communication open. You will need to be able to tolerate uncomfortable truths and work together to reconcile them as no one person is solely responsible for the health of your union;

• Protect your union from outside influences. This can be in-laws, extracurricular activities, work, children, even your own mental health. Stay vigilant and address anything that threatens your union;

• Have FUN! It is your job to intentionally invest the time, energy and resources in keeping your marriage fun.

Stay tuned because we, too, are committed to grow through play. We have learned to make every day our playground!

REFLECTIONS

REFLECTIONS

JUST LIKE GOD PLANNED

Min. Taiwan Simmons

JUST LIKE GOD PLANNED

Min. Taiwan Simmons

"For I know the thoughts that I think toward you, saith the LORD, thoughts of peace, and not of evil, to give you an expected end."
Jeremiah 29:11

Twenty-eight years ago, I met the love of my life. My best friend. My lover. My toughest critic. My biggest fan. We do everything together. We choose to do life together and enjoy being around each other ... most of the time.

It wasn't always like that. When we first met, we were both broken and running from our lives. We were each other's escape. I'm sure that Sh'nai will have her own perspective on this, but for me, Sh'nai was an answered prayer, a commitment to God, and a reminder that even though you may go through some rough seasons, and tough patches, there is and can be joy on the other side. So, this is my version of our love story. I'm going to cover love, business, and the unique dynamics of our marriage from my point of view. I'm going to express to you why I know without a shadow of a doubt that everything that has happened up until this point has been ordained by God. That alone makes it worth it to me. In other words, I know that I am operating under a promise! Be advised, what you are about to read just might change your life!

If you asked me 30 years ago if I could imagine what I have now, I would have laughed in your face. Married with children and with the same woman?

"Never that!" I would have said to you.

I wasn't looking for anything committed. I was looking for a good time. So, when I met Sh'nai initially, the idea of being married and raising a family were all new and scary to me. I was too busy sneaking into her dorm room and playing house. After I got through the good time, of course, and began to get serious, well, I'll explain this in further detail a little later. Some may ask why I had this filter. Why was I not interested in the whole commitment thing? Here's why:

By the time I was 14, my parents repeatedly rejected me and due to making such poor choices, I was raised by my Great Grandmother. Sound familiar? Some of you reading now can relate. Talk about a blessing in disguise! Little did I know, Mother, which is what we all called her, would instill many of the values in my life that are near and dear to me today, and that have shaped who I have become. This is the grown me talking now. Back then, I was only trying to survive and feel loved.

Rejection is a difficult thing, and when you experience that from your parents, as I did, it causes growing pains. I was depressed, had low self-esteem, and even though Mother would always speak into my life, I didn't want that from her. I wanted that kind of love and affirmation from my parents.

"Man, I can see it. When you grow up, you're going to be something special!"

She would say these sorts of things to me all the time. I smiled and thanked her because I appreciated my great-grandma, but she didn't understand. She was already almost 70! What could she possibly know about what I was going through? I didn't think she could relate or understand. My stay with Ella Bennett (Mother) was off and on from the age of two. The first time was after a fight between mom and dad that landed him in jail, and mom in a mental health institution. Like clockwork, my mom would get back on her feet, come and take me from Mother, stop taking her medicine and I would end up back with Mother again. It was a painful cycle.

My life was a mess and all I could think about was what if; what if my life was like other families I saw? That was not my reality, though. I now know that she did understand, and these were all seeds that were being planted and that God had a plan for them later in my life.

Things began to shift for me right around the end of eighth grade. I was 13 and because of a conversation that I had with my cousin's girlfriend, I decided to focus on creating a better version of me. I transformed myself from the chubby guy with low self-esteem who didn't care about much of anything into a fit, high energy, self-confident athletic stud who was not going to let his parents' mistakes and the previous hand he was dealt determine his life. So, in about six months' time, the results and changes were so noticeable that the neighborhood bullies began to get jealous, and girls noticed. This was exactly what I needed to focus on feeling better about myself and less on the pain of my parents' rejection. I loved the attention that I was getting, and for the next three and a half years, my ministry was me. I became active in sports and started having sex. If social media, smartphones and apps were available back then, I would be famous for all the wrong reasons! I was running 100 miles per hour and there was no end in sight. That's the way I wanted it, or so I thought.

High school was a breeze. By the time I was a senior, no one was telling jokes about me. All the superficial work I'd done on myself was paying off. When I graduated, I was one of the most popular guys at the school. While I was there, I was active; sports, school committees, girls. I was able to hide my pain by masking it with poor choices. Back then, I didn't understand the spiritual consequences of the choices I was making. I just wanted to feel good. I just wanted to fit in and be accepted. No one taught me how to love myself or how to deal with my emotions. I'd already learned not to ask for help when I was younger, so there was no need to ask now. I thought I had it all under control.

Going from high school to college was going to be a breeze, too, I thought. I was dealt an immediate reality check. I never even thought that I would get to college when I was a kid. I didn't even know about the SAT until I was in 10th grade. As a result, I was unprepared for college-level work. Remember, I lived with my great-grandmother, and then my grandmother, who I moved in with during high school because she was closer to school. What did they know about algebra, and trigonometry? So, my college career started in college prep. I had to take remedial classes as a part of my necessary admission process to the college I attended. It felt like another rejection. Another disappointment. I was going to handle this the same way I handled everything else: I focused on myself and found an outlet with women at the school. I was once again able to hide the pain and the disappointments of my life.

At this point, many of you may be asking what does any of this have to do with love, business, and marriage? It has everything to do with it! Let me explain. When I met my wife, all of this is who I brought to our relationship.

My dysfunction, my disappointments, my lack of self-esteem, and my fears. These were all a part of the filters that I saw life through, and they all contributed to the way I interacted with Sh'nai, received from Sh'nai, and thought about our relationship. Here is the other thing that I brought to the relationship: choices. Every choice has a consequence, good, bad, or indifferent. Make a choice, and there will be an immediate or eventual outcome. This became glaringly obvious when we first began dating. I decided that I would commit to our relationship. The problem was that my choices were following me and interfering with our relationship. Girls would call the dorm pay phone (remember pay phones?) and ask for Sh'nai, then say disrespectful things to her or about me.

"Girl, do you think he's gonna be faithful to you?" or "He's a hoe, are you sure you want to get with him?"

I even tried to give up at one point. There is so much more that I could say about this season that led up to this point in my life. You will have to purchase my personal project for that.

Okay, so now you have the context. You have a snapshot of who I was entering my marriage. We dated for two years, and we both had distractions that allowed us to not have to deal with our past stuff. We were working on rescuing her siblings from the state system and dealing with the loss of a child. This was while we were still in college, looking for a place, taking finals, traveling back-and-forth from Buffalo to New York City, and it just made sense for us to tie the knot. So, we did. How many people do you know that have done what appeared to be the right thing for the wrong reason? Don't mistake what I'm saying. I was going to marry Sh'nai. I just wish that I had been more prepared when I did. I had no idea what a healthy relationship looked like. Sh'nai brought her own stuff into the relationship, as well. Now we had to make this work.

LOVE

I loved Sh'nai to the best of my ability and knowledge. My only frame of reference was Mother, who took in everyone and gave everything she had. So, I thought, "I can do that." A near death experience when I was a child and a personal encounter with the devil instilled an understanding of faith in me that I brought to the marriage. I was the faith leader in our relationship and have always been. I did my best to show Sh'nai that I loved her. I gave everything I had. Despite my greatest attempts, I failed miserably!

We succeeded in removing Sh'nai's siblings from the system. In addition to our 2-year-old son and newborn daughter, we were suddenly a family of six. I was working ridiculous hours. Remember those choices that I mentioned earlier on? Well, many of those choices that we made caused us to be in debt and we had to deal with the consequences. The new car smell had worn off. Now we had to be grownups.

You may have heard the saying: "Strangers passing in the night"? Well, that's what we were. I worked overnight, and when I arrived home around 8 a.m., Sh'nai would pass the babies to me and leave for work to get there by nine. When she got in from work, I would pass her the babies and go to sleep to be ready for my graveyard shift. This was our life. When I was not being pulled into mandatory overtime and we actually got a day off together, we caught up on family stuff; paying bills, shopping for food so we didn't all starve, paying bills (this is not a typo). There was just not enough time to address everything. Most importantly, our marriage came in last place. We were not connecting, and when we did it was mostly surface. Why get deep when we had all of these other things to hide behind? So, that's what we did. Eventually, because of the lack of connection between us, including intimacy that goes deeper than sex, there was infidelity. It was the biggest mistake of my life. Here I was, this guy who was the faith leader in our home and I messed up. My faith in God, everything Mother taught me, and my love for Sh'nai wasn't enough.

BUSINESS

Business saved my marriage! After my infidelity, our marriage was on fumes. We made a promise when we took our vows to hang in there til death do us part, but candidly speaking, I had no clue how we were going to recover. Initially, we did what came naturally. We found a way to bury the hurt and focus on something else. This time, it was our faith. We decided that we needed a better relationship with Christ. Then one day, during a rough season financially, we were down to $11. We needed food in the house. There was no way we could feed a whole family for very long with that, even 25 years ago. The car had just broken down and barely made it back to the house from work. We decided to use our new understanding about the power of faith, touching and agreement, so we prayed over the car, over that $11, and we were off to the supermarket.

God showed up! We were able to get groceries, and as we were thanking God and trying to understand what happened, the car shut down at a stoplight. Again, I thought, how am I going to solve this issue? After what felt like 10 minutes, but was only really two, I mustered up the strength to walk into what appeared to be a bar. By strength, I mean pride. It's a man thing, having to swallow it and ask for help again was grueling. And this was on top of the fact that our finances were not good at the time and we were in recovery mode in our relationship.

It was winter in Buffalo, freezing and snowing, and I swallowed what pride I had left and asked if anyone could give me a jump. A gentleman immediately offered to assist and five minutes after connecting his battery to ours, the car was working again. Sh'nai and I both thanked him, thinking, man, this faith thing really works! So, I put the car in drive and then we were on our way, or so we thought. The car shut off again!

I had to go back into that bar and ask again! I was frozen, could not feel any of my extremities, and I was really struggling with the embarrassment of the situation. What a loser I am, I thought. How could I have allowed my family to be in this situation? This is not the life I had wanted for them, or myself. In James 4: 10 (KJV), it says: "Humble yourselves in the sight of the Lord and He shall lift you up." Looking back on this situation, as embarrassed as I was, I had no other choice. I went back in. I humbled myself again. I could see the slight irritation on the man's face. As we were pulling out the cables again, he suggested we leave the cables on a little longer to be sure we could get home. Then he asked, "Have you ever looked for ways to make additional income?"

Now, wait a minute. This was 1997, so multi-level marketing and home-based businesses were fresh and new for many. I was indebted and intrigued. I had just had a pity party with God and shared my frustrations. Could this be what this was all about in the first place? I 100% believe it was. After we returned home, Sh'nai and I had a brief discussion about the opportunity, and we were in! Little did we know that later this decision would be the glue that kept our marriage together. We connected on so many different levels. We were working together to build wealth and get free from the very things that contributed to the bad choices we made. This was something bigger than both of us! Working for ourselves meant that we made our own hours, we decided who to work with, and we got to work with other successful business people. This was all so new to us. We had never experienced married couples working together to build anything. Not only that, but these couples were also believers, and they were not bashful about their love for God and how important their faith was in their businesses and in their relationships. We spent as much time with them as we could. We watched how they worked together, we asked questions, and the law of environment kicked in.

I love John Maxwell's definition: To grow to our full potential, we have to be in the right environment. Growth thrives in favorable conditions. You and I grow the most when we surround ourselves with people and opportunities conducive to our development."

I could not have said it better myself. Some of these couples began to mentor us, and we learned amazing principles about life, love, business, and marriage.

We traveled all over the country building our business together, children in tow. We did whatever it took to make it work because we were determined to succeed. And we did it together. I know that this was God's purpose for that cold, snowy day in Buffalo, NY. This is what saved our marriage and laid the foundation for the work that we do today.

MARRIAGE

There were so many lessons that we learned during those first years together; communication, sacrifice, patience, and compromise were just a few. It wasn't perfect, but we were committed to making us work. We were going to keep our marriage vows because, for us, divorce was never an option. While we were working the business and restoring our relationship, we never lost our senses of humor. Raising teenagers and toddlers at the same time had a lot to do with it, I'm sure. It was either lose our minds because of juggling everything or figure out a way to make it all not so serious. That was more of a task for Sh'nai as the more serious one in our relationship. Not now! As we grew closer, we began to balance each other out. I began to identify a sterner side and Sh'nai began to unleash her inner comedian. We would have family game nights and dance contests with the kids; karaoke, Uno, anything that made us feel free and connected, not just to our kids, but to each other. We were often taken back to the days in the college dorms when we just met and played together and had a good time. It was also right around this time that we were growing in our faith.

We relocated from New York to Virginia and were serious about God. As we were growing in our understanding of our marriage, God began to pull distressed marriages to us. It seemed like a coincidence at first. I would meet someone who happened to be married and as we began to talk, he shared the challenges that he was having in his marriage. I wondered why is he sharing such personal details? Then God said, "I've called you to this ministry because of what I've brought you through. Now that you are qualified, you can help heal other marriages." I remember the first time I shared what God said to me: right after we had a crazy assignment with a pastor and his wife. Guess what their issue was? That's right. Infidelity! Sh'nai and I both heard from God during this season, and it was the foundation of what we have today.

1 Cor 13: 4-8 gives a powerful definition of love. Without preaching as I wrap up this chapter, love is everything you need to be successful in business and marriage, but not small, self-involved love. In ourselves, we are incapable. Our past experiences and choices hold us hostage if we don't have something greater to reach for. The love Sh'nai and I have for each other only became enough when we began to love something greater than ourselves.

The combination of God and business saved our marriage because we reached for legacy after first reaching for God. Now marriage is our burn. We accepted the call from God. We are committed to help restore and fuel marriages to not make the same mistakes and choices we made.

Our company, Playfuelled Marriages, focuses on helping couples grow through play. With our experiences and spiritual, professional and clinical expertise, we provide unique experiences for married couples designed to help them rekindle the passion and fun that they lost or fail to prioritize in their relationship. Every couple walks away with tangible, right-now skills that will help their marriage succeed. It is our prayer and desire, as well as our personal mission, that every couple enjoy a playfuelled marriage!

REFLECTIONS

REFLECTIONS

SECOND TIME AROUND

Tamara Mitchell-Davis

SECOND TIME AROUND

Tamara Mitchell-Davis

A good marriage isn't something you find, it's something you make and you have to keep on making it.

Before I jump into the present, allow me to give you a bit of backstory as to how this is my second time around with marriage. My second husband and I first met and dated over 27 years ago. We went our separate ways, married, tended to life, divorced, and started communicating again.

We reconnected when he was on the brink of coming home from federal prison. I wasn't concerned about him selling me promises and broken dreams—commonly referred to as "jail talk" because I wasn't looking for a relationship. I was quite fine being single and finding my way back to self—self-love and self-awareness—and was solely focused on raising my daughters, which meant starting all over from ground zero after a divorce.

I remember going to my mom's house one day after work, and my now-husband was on the phone. He'd always kept in touch with members of my family. While married, I stood clear of him. I mean, I left him for a reason when we dated before, so I was not interested in opening that door again, let alone communicating with him.

However, I felt he knew me, knew how I was, and I was looking for someone to remind me of that because I felt lost. I felt like a failure, to be honest. Divorced, bankrupt, jobless, and looking for validation because somehow, over the previous 10+ years, I had lost myself.

I didn't know if God was sending a message my way or if it was the trick of the enemy. All I know is that I wanted to feel whole as I pieced my life back together. The first time I heard his voice on the phone, it was like time stood still. He had the same smooth voice and that relaxed, cool demeanor. We talked fast and briefly because there was a short amount of time available on the phone. He asked if he could call me back another time and I agreed.

From that moment on, we started communicating more frequently on the phone and in letters. He sent a picture of himself, and he had dreads in his hair but his face was the same. So much had changed while we were apart. He had lost his young son to gun violence, and I had lost family members who he was very fond of. We would reminisce on the phone for about 10 minutes every other day. A few months in, he asked if I would visit him and I said yes.

I will never forget my first visit. For one, it was a 3-to four-hour drive to get to him and there were certain colors you could not wear. I had on a pair of navy blue capri jeans, a white shirt with silver writing that had the words love on it, and silver sandals. He had on a khaki outfit and black boots. When he walked into the visiting room, I was sitting down in the chair. Our eyes connected as he was walking closer and closer and we both started crying, more like sobbing. We had a short embrace because you couldn't hold and hug for too long and we sat down and just cried some more. We had more time to reflect on life face-to-face; all of our losses, wins, mistakes, hurdles, and what we desired. I asked him what he remembered about me. His response: "You was always independent, strong willed, old soul, good heart and a strong person." Hearing how he saw me, I wondered how I felt so lost and broken, sitting in the visiting room with him. The visit was filled with laughter, tears, and some silence. It was not an awkward silence but a peaceful silence. We agreed to keep talking, but I also advised him that I wasn't interested in a relationship due to our past and abrupt breakup.

We broke up because of his lifestyle and my unwillingness to partake in the shenanigans. He was well-liked and I felt it was difficult for him to be a one-woman man, so I left him. Over time, I feel I had forgiven him and forgotten some of what transpired between us. I wasn't holding anything over his head, and because we both had gone our separate ways and then connected again, in my opinion, there was no bad blood or unresolved issues that we had to work through. Besides, we were just friends.

Well, fast forward, we continued to communicate and opened ourselves up to love again. We had lived a little, and I believe we both wanted change and were willing to see what would come out of it. This meant taking a chance, taking a risk on love. I strongly believe there are things a married man or woman should not do or situations a married man or woman should not find him or herself in. Things can be taken way out of context and we would bump heads about this. He felt I didn't trust him, but I had no reason not to. What happened between us in the past was old. We came together with a new, fresh, clean slate, in my eyes. If I didn't trust him, I would not be with him this time.

We only ran into a problem when he gave me a reason to question his actions. His way of thinking was different from my way of thinking; his way of thinking was I know how far to go, and my way of thinking is don't open the door for people to assume or think they could walk right on in because women will do that. Because of this, we found ourselves in marriage counseling and, at one point, on the brink of separating because things and women from his past were now in my present. I refused to settle or operate with loose boundaries, people attributed my feelings to him not being able to speak to women or me being controlling, which is absurd and far from the truth. If I am committed, I could never have another man thinking or feeling he has access to me or to think there's a possibility. I had left my previous marriage and I had it in my head that if we stayed together, great, and if things didn't work out, at least we tried. I was not compromising my standards or my peace of mind since I had gained it back and leaving him was an option that I had no problem exploring. My husband didn't get it until I asked him one question, "Would you want me having extra communications with other men, strictly platonic or not?" He said he did not. I believe it was at that moment when we started being on the same page because he understood my point of view. It baffles me how it took one question for him to have a light bulb moment. Don't do to me what you wouldn't want me to do to you. Things can start off innocent and lead into other things. I wouldn't and didn't want to risk that and I hoped he didn't want that either.

I didn't see healthy marriages modeled in my family or in my community. My mother never married. My father married and divorced three times, and my grandparents were married a long time but there was never a display of affection. As a matter of fact, I don't even recall seeing my grandparents speak, be affectionate with one another, or think they enjoyed each other's company. I guess back in the day people stayed married because they honored their vows, for the children, or other arrangements and reasons. I mean, it was evident they were intimate because they had children together, but I never saw love or communication demonstrated. I never aspired to grow up and get married until I saw The Cosby Show on television, and even that family dynamic seemed unreal. Yet, there we were, two people with baggage trying to love and make sense of life together. Was I looking for a happily-ever-after love story? And, if I was, what's wrong with that? I was torn between settling for whatever and turning down my dreams because I was considered unrealistic.

I expressed to him that I had changed. I was not the young woman he was with back in the day with no children. I had children, goals, dreams, standards, and I wanted something different for me and my daughters. What I settled for before wasn't something I was willing to do now. Life changed me. This time around, I wasn't taking any shorts or dealing with any of his BS.

Our different approaches to talking about all the things married people need to talk about made me think my husband was emotionally unavailable to me. He wanted to provide, and if he felt like he wasn't providing or appreciated, he would seem distant. I didn't like this feeling because I wanted us to plan and work together. I wanted him to know I had his back and needed to know he had mine. I wanted to feel protected. Finally, we started talking more about why we both acted or reacted in certain ways. Expressing my feelings came easy if I was angry, upset, or combative, but I needed to be understood, valued, and appreciated. My husband is non-confrontational and would rather not deal with a situation, let things go. I prefer to meet issues head-on. Therefore, it's definitely been a dance trying to find our own rhythm. We came back together with baggage from our respective relationships and experiences but rekindled feelings for each other trying to sort through life. We agreed to have each other's back and put each other first. Yet, our lines of communication kept getting crossed and I felt he lacked boundaries when it came to women from his past. I call him Mr. Sunshine because he is so friendly and always turning a positive from a negative. Everything he promised to do when we got back together, he has done. But I also felt my happiness was an afterthought for him. Getting raw and honest with one another helped us work through that patch.

Words matter, and the lack of words does matter too. As we had gotten through some initial hurdles, I never questioned my husband's support. Whenever we both attempted different business ventures, we supported each other, but I needed more because he thought his physical presence was enough. I wanted his emotional and mental support, too. I was physically supportive of him and tried to provide emotional and mental support, but he's not a talker, so I would get frustrated and shut down. He felt that I was angry when I wasn't. I just withdrew into a cocoon to protect my feelings. As I was digging more and more into the business to stay out of his way, my husband was feeling neglected. I remember one night, I was in the office working when he went to bed and popped his head in and said, "Don't forget about me." I didn't think anything of it until he started making more and more frequent comments when I was in my office for a long time. In my head, I was staying out the way when he wanted me in his way. Again, this goes back to communication, but it takes two. It was up to the both of us to figure out how to manage love, marriage, and the business.

I don't think my husband understood the impact of the business or even what I was doing in the office until he was at my first conference in person. He saw for himself, up close and personal, what I was building. I believe it gave him a different appreciation as he supported me physically and learned to support me emotionally. He would ask me how things were going. If I was in my office working, he brought me dinner and made sure I was straight and I am so appreciative of that. This also made me more conscious of my time because I never wanted him to feel neglected. I worked in the office while he was at work on the weekends. If I came home from work and needed to get some work done, I gave myself a time limit by setting my alarm until it went off. If he needed my attention for something, I would make a conscious effort to be present. We agreed to do the same for each other.

Effective communication has been our challenge because it's easy to be on one accord when you are able to express how you feel. The challenging part is being open and receptive when you have to discuss the hard stuff. My husband feels that he's not a complainer and allows things to go. While that might be great, it's important in marriage to express yourself whether things are going good or not so good, and when you lack the ability to do either, you can experience problems in your relationship. My husband felt I was complaining if I spoke up about something that bothered me. I wanted us both to be able to share with each other openly instead of being silent and letting things build. Eventually, he came around, but it took time for us to build up to this space.

Here's how we started doing things differently:

- Trust that we had each other's best interest at heart. We needed to have a level of understanding with one another and safe space for vulnerability to openly express our feelings. This is a work in progress area for us.

- Small thoughtful acts. I know him bringing me dinner while working or him being at my events was his way of showing me love and support. I was looking for him to ask questions, to be connected with what I was doing and be part of the business, not just physically present. Me calling him throughout the day, making dinner, and ensuring that I made time for him was my way of showing love and support. Once we started getting on the same page, the smoother things seemed to be. That included being more affectionate with each other and not being routine, going through the motions.

- No secrets. We share openly and have tough conversations when necessary. However, this has been the most challenging area because you never know how it will be received by the other person and the outcome. We can only hope for the best.

- Focus on our common goals and be willing to try new things to keep our love and marriage fun and spicy. It still takes two willing individuals to do this. We went to counseling for a while and stopped. That was a mistake. Counseling allowed us to learn more about each other, ourselves and coping skills when challenges arose. It is something to continue and that's what we plan to do.

- Respect each other. We are individuals with separate brains, likes, dislikes, pasts, hangups, habits, etc. Respect the position of each other to lovingly agree and disagree.

We are two imperfect people and, at the time, we were searching for peace, happiness, love, stability, and support. We reunited with NOTHING and started building brick by brick. And to think, we almost walked away from what we've built with one another because we spoke different love languages and the signals kept getting crossed. There is a saying that "love wins". I do believe it wholeheartedly but I also feel that marriage requires more than love to be present. Not just words spoken but also actions.

One of the songs during our reception was "Second Time Around," by Shalimar. We believe God brought us back together for a reason. We've had a lot of give-and-take over the years, and it's been pretty good since we got over most of the obstacles and are still working through them. The reality is no one is perfect and nothing is perfect, but because I can say the good and the great definitely outweigh the bad, I believe we're headed down the right path.

Having a business or marriage doesn't automatically fix problems, heal trauma or break habits. Addressing the issues, communicating, wanting change, doing the work and leading with love are key essentials to making it all work.

REFLECTIONS

REFLECTIONS

A CHANGED MAN

Joe Davis (JD)

A CHANGED MAN

Joe Davis (JD)

Who the son sets free is free indeed ~ John 8:36

Growing up, people saw me as a problem child. As a young kid I made bad choices. I started running the streets and going between my mother's house and my aunt's house, which was my go-to when I was in trouble. I had no strong male guidance and was doing all the wrong things. I became hard to handle because you couldn't tell me anything. I mean, nothing. I felt like I knew it all and skipped right to dabbling in the fast life to make money: selling drugs, and other criminal activity that landed me in jail for stretches of time.

I've spent the majority of my life in and out of jail: shackles, solitary confinement, limited phone calls, and zero access to the real world. I slowly adapted to the consequences of my decisions. Forty-plus years later, I was sitting in a federal penitentiary being sick and tired of the same old routine (freedom, work, jail). I was determined to do things differently. Was this because I was incarcerated or did I really mean it this time? I am a true believer in the man upstairs (God) and He knew my heart. He knew I wanted to make a change. So He brought the Queen (my wife) back into my life. It is my life experiences that brought me to write this chapter on how I view and move through love, business, and marriage.

I was familiar with the business part. In 1998, before my final stint in prison, I started an organization called JD Enterprise that focused on inner city kids (kids at risk). I was once one of those kids. I played sports and have always been a sports fan, so I started a basketball league through JD Enterprise. Our basketball games were held at Waverly Park in Hartford and even featured in Source magazine. Although I was in the streets, I came up under my idol, Ms. Bethea. She helped so many kids in sports and in academics and provided them with an outlet to steer them toward something different than getting in trouble. Ms.

Bethea taught me the game, and I told her I wanted to start my own basketball league because she was ready to retire. She told me to run with it and that's what I did. I wanted to bring something different to our city to provide fun and a safe sport that could attract a crowd and do what Ms. Bethea did for so many children and for so many years. I wanted to make Waverly Park better than it was, to turn it up a notch, and the opportunity was basketball games. Starting JD Enterprise was a way to put my money into something legal. I hired people in the community to be referees, a DJ, and we had our own hype man. A local business, Exclusive Linez, created banners and basketball jerseys for the teams. It was the best thing that I could have ever started on my own. The love and passion that I have for sports, basketball being one of my favorites, is what made me go even harder to bring the dream to reality.

I brought Rucker basketball to Connecticut. Now, for the people that don't know, Rucker is a summer basketball tournament played in Harlem, New York. This is where the best street players, occasional members of the NBA, and some of the top ranked college players would play to show off their talent. Players had uniforms, we had a live DJ, a comedian, and an announcer to call the game. I had 19 teams in the league the first and second year, and 21 teams the final years; (15 adult teams and 6 youth teams). I had four successful years with both men and young boys, and I would have kept going but one of my referees got shot by someone shooting from the woods that surrounded the park. People didn't feel safe. For once, I felt like I was making a good contribution to society, and I felt really good about doing something positive for a change. I started a business from nothing, I had sponsors, and I was running an organization that was seen as a positive contribution to our community. Everything seemed to be going great, but things started turning again for me, in a bad way.

An old acquaintance approached me with a deal that, for some reason, I could not refuse. It seemed to be such a quick job and easy money, your mother could have pulled it off. But dealing with the wrong people landed me back in jail again in 2004 with a six-year federal prison bid. This time, prison really broke me mentally.

I felt a million miles away. Two years after my sentencing, I called home and got some disturbing news. My youngest child (who has a twin) had been shot dead. My whole world caved in when I got that information. He was a great kid who had good grades, played sports, and was loved by everyone. He was an innocent bystander. That was the worst time of my life. I stopped eating, and I struggled to keep my sanity. I just wanted to die and give up because I blamed myself for not being home to protect my son. The thoughts that ran through my mind and the guilt that consumed me had me feeling lower than low. And although I considered checking out physically, on the flipside, I felt it would have been selfish because I was only thinking of myself. I had my son's twin sister, my older children, my grandkids, and other family members still here.

I eventually picked my head up and started praying for forgiveness, peace, and understanding. I had to stay strong and remember that I was God's child and He got me through that dark period of time. You know in the Bible it says God won't put more on you than you can bear. I had to keep reminding myself of that even through the tears.

You know you can have all the money in the world but money doesn't mean anything when you can't do anything with it. Money couldn't bring my son back. Money couldn't heal my heart. Money didn't make me magically free or be a support to my children and family. I chased money all my life, but there I was in Kansas, Missouri, feeling hopeless and helpless. It's a hurt feeling when you lose your child and you can't do anything, not even be present for the funeral. My last memory of him was on a videotape lying in a casket. I don't like talking or thinking about it. I've come to grips with his loss but it brings me to a very emotional state of mind. Because of all of this, plus the fact that I was still in the system, I made up my mind and said enough is enough. I knew God had a better way for me. I wanted something different for myself, and a better relationship with my children. Both had been strained and difficult to manage because I was in and out of jail.

That's a bit of my backstory, but how I ended up writing a chapter about love and marriage is because God reconnected me to the woman who has always held a piece of my heart. He knew who I needed. We dated 28 plus years ago when I was in the street life. She was tired of dealing with my bullshit, and we eventually parted ways because of it. I let her go and didn't fight for her or our relationship because as a street dude, I had too much pride to actually show her how I felt about her. She had my nose wide open, and to me, that was not who Joe Davis was.

We went our separate ways, married other people, experienced divorce, and reconnected right when I was about to come home from prison. I was always connected with her family, but she avoided me because, at the time, she was in a relationship. I heard she was back single, and on a whim, I called her mom, and she was at the house. We only talked for a few minutes because when you're incarcerated, you only get a few minutes of phone time. She gave me her condolences and cried and prayed with me over the loss of my son. Although it was never our intention to get back together, we started talking more frequently. I made up my mind when I came home that I was going to prove to her that I was a changed man and never stopped loving her. I never wanted her to leave me the first time, so I know God was on his job working on me to be the man that was gonna be there for her.

During the whole time of transitioning back into society, I was trying to prove that she didn't make a mistake with me. Although I had the business thing down from before I went to Missouri, by the time I got home, the world had changed. I felt like a fish out of water trying to get familiar with life outside of the penitentiary.

When I got home, I looked for a job but went about it the wrong way. I talked with someone from my past who I had no business talking to about anything, but I was focused on proving to my then girlfriend (now wife) that I was serious. What I failed to do was tell her who was helping me look for a job. Strike number one.

When she found out, how she viewed me and even trusted me took a hit. Then there were other women numbers in my phone. I kept telling her it was nothing and tried to prove to her that I was telling the truth and didn't want anyone but her, but she didn't believe me. The trust window was slowly closing.

I realized I went about things in the wrong way, but my focus was on getting a job to help pay bills because I never wanted her to feel as if I was lazy and using her. Things between us got complicated because her trust with me was compromised.

To give you some history, this is my third marriage. The previous marriages failed because I was a hustler, spent too much time incarcerated, and didn't see another way outside being in the life. Returning back to a relationship I once had, I never wanted my past to stunt my wife's growth. I came into the marriage with baggage but I was determined to get on the right path and head in a better direction. We found a church home and I knew I'd change. I was singing in the men's choir and was being obedient to the Word of God. Anything I did, I did with my wife because I just didn't want to be in the wrong place at the wrong time with the wrong person because I got away with so much in the past. God had spared my life so many times already.

Now that big word—TRUST—I would like to talk about what that means to me. My word was my bond because when you don't have your word, or bond, you don't have trust. I'm from the old school, but my wife—who really loves me—is several years younger, and our generations think differently because we grew up in different eras. I'm not saying that age made a huge difference, but when I got home, I became so focused on getting that money without coming out of my character. I was working multiple jobs, sometimes too many jobs, simultaneously to make ends meet. I felt good about being able to financially contribute to our lives, but in the course of me doing that, I lost sight of my wife. That was not a good feeling for her. She started doing her thing, writing books and running her business, so I thought we were good. What I didn't realize is that she wanted me right there and connected with her: mentally, emotionally and physically. I was so focused on trying to prove that her time wasn't being wasted that I somewhat lost my way. We were like ships passing in the night, and I wasn't in tune with her needs. My whole focus was work, get this money, work, get this money so I could contribute something to the household. I could feel the distance with her starting as she found ways to occupy herself since I was working so much. I didn't want any more BS in my life and I didn't want to lose her again.

In previous relationships, when I worked a million jobs and dabbled in street life to take care of my family, there came a point where I didn't feel appreciated anymore. It was all about what I could do or give. I made up my mind to not go back in the streets this time around because I didn't want to repeat the same thing again. I felt the only way to contribute was to prove to her that I was not lazy and I wanted to pay my way. She is the breadwinner, and that bothered me because I've always had it to give before. That's what a man is supposed to do.

My wife is my heart and a true goal getter. I didn't want her to stop me, and I didn't want to stop her from pursuing her own hopes and dreams. So I stood back and let her do her thing because I never wanted to be the cause or reason why she didn't pursue her dreams. She took a chance on me again and I didn't want her to regret it. Once she is focused on something, she will work and work and work some more, so I experienced some lonely nights.

I had plenty of nights when I went to sleep and she wasn't in the bed because she was working, out of state on trips, attending conferences, and I didn't want to stop her. She wanted me to go, and my response would always be, "Baby, I need to work and get this money." I didn't realize that, yet again, I became focused on the money part. It wasn't until she brought it to my attention and after we had a big argument that our relationship was becoming more strained. I think she was wondering why this was happening and questioning trust again, and I was concerned with bringing money to the table to help with bills. We tried counseling a few times and I came up with the idea of starting a couples chat. I thought it would help me learn from other couples and vice versa, but it was inconsistent and I stopped pushing for it to happen.

Having an age difference and coming from separate yet similar worlds, we tend to view things differently. I am more laid back and reserved because I feel like I've been there, done that, and I bring wisdom to the table. She is younger, spontaneous, and more outgoing.

I loved her from the beginning. I loved her in the middle and I'm going to love her until I die. I love her wholeheartedly, but communication was a bit challenging for me. She wanted me to talk about how I feel, and I wasn't used to that. She wanted to plan together and be on the same page, and I wasn't used to that either. Most everything with her was new to me because I wasn't used to being open and talking about everything from the serious to the silly.

She calls me Mr. Sunshine because I always try to bring something positive to a negative situation. Whether it's with me and her or with someone else, I think before I speak now more than ever before. In the past, I was a hot head and now I am so calm. I think people take my kindness for weakness or me being delayed, as if something is wrong with me intellectually. I am more patient and I try to give people the benefit of the doubt. I thought by supporting my wife and her dreams, staying out her way would give her the time and space to handle her business. She would say she was feeling overwhelmed, and I thought she was worried about money because I was used to having a lot of it. In fact, she was looking for me to take some things off her plate, to be present and emotionally available, but I didn't see it that way. She stayed in her office, and I stayed in my man cave. The routine was work, home, sex, sleep. No pillow talk because we were too tired to talk.

The young lady I met before and am married to now is so intelligent, beautiful, radiant, smart, and spunky, and she still has my nose wide open. That's how good she is. She turned me out but I still had a street mentality that conflicted with the love that she has for me.

Marriage, from my perspective, takes two people truly devoted to one another. When there's no communication and trust, the marriage starts to decline. I was open to trying therapy to breathe life back into us and reconnect in my marriage. If there's no love in the relationship, how can it be a loving marriage? If there's no verbal communication, how can you be on the same page with business? You need to have understanding for both to work in love, business and ultimately marriage.

I may be wrong, but I'm only human and just going on based on what I've learned and experienced. We got married for better or worse, meaning it's going to be some rough points in a relationship. Communication is key, and I don't want my wife to think I've taken her, her love, or our marriage for granted. I want her to love me for me and be proud of the man that I am and have evolved into.

I honestly didn't think I could write this chapter, but my wife encouraged me that I could just by sharing my wisdom from my own viewpoint, past and present. I must say as I close, if there's no communication, trust and no understanding, finding love in the marriage could be hard. And when you add in business, that's another layer that has the possibility of hurting or helping the relationship depending on the two individuals involved.

I realized that I had to be attentive to my wife's needs. I had to put her first. I had to learn to be emotionally present for her, not just physically present, and I am still working on this. Because we come from two different backgrounds and generations, I have to also take that into account.

When we came back together, I was determined to have our wedding as an all-white affair because it's the symbol of purity. There had been so much darkness in my life that I was viewing my marriage as another chance to get things right. She came back in my life when I was down and out so I do believe she was sent by God. Because I believe this, I choose to live as a different man; as a loving husband and a better father to the best of my ability. I'm not perfect, and I may not always get it right but at least I am trying. I am free from shame. I am free from my past. I am free from trying to prove my worth.

Things don't just happen overnight. It takes time and patience. You are required to put pride to the side and fight for what you want in life whether it's love, business, marriage, or all three.

A woman can't change a man because she loves him, a man changes himself because he loves her!

REFLECTIONS

REFLECTIONS

GUIDED REFLECTIONS

REFLECTIONS

What are areas of challenge in your marriage and/or business?

_____
_____
_____
_____
_____
_____
_____
_____
_____
_____
_____
_____
_____

REFLECTIONS

REFLECTIONS

What are opportunities for growth in your marriage and/or business?

_____
_____
_____
_____
_____
_____
_____
_____
_____
_____
_____
_____
_____
_____
_____

REFLECTIONS

REFLECTIONS

Based on what you've read, what are you willing to commit to in order to bring about change in your marriage and/or business?

_____
_____
_____
_____
_____
_____
_____
_____
_____
_____
_____
_____
_____
_____

REFLECTIONS

REFLECTIONS

What areas do you need to explore for support and assistance?

_____
_____
_____
_____
_____
_____
_____
_____
_____
_____
_____
_____
_____
_____

REFLECTIONS

MEET THE AUTHORS

Catherine
Latoya Grant-Alston

Catherine Latoya Grant-Alston is an international award-winning entrepreneur and corporate practitioner as well as an Amazon best-selling author. She is the CEO and co-founder of ART Financial Solutions, LLC d/b/a Alston Kingdom specializing in personal and business financial coaching, strategic vision planning, and treasury technology for corporations. ART Financial Solutions, LLC services the community and educational organizations by providing financial literacy, coaching, and training through the Alston Kingdom lifestyle brand.

Catherine Latoya holds a Bachelor of Science in Business Administration from the University of Connecticut as well as a Master of Business Administration from the University of Massachusetts. She has worked in the financial industry for more than 20 years and is the recipient of many industry awards including ACHI Magazine Award, 100 Women of Color, Alexander Hamilton Award, and TMI Treasury Team of the Year Award to name a few.

She believes in community and continuously provides financial and educational services to individuals, organizations, and corporations to increase global financial knowledge. Catherine Latoya is an active member of Delta Sigma Theta Sorority, Incorporated. She lives in Connecticut with her husband Reggie and their 2 children.

You can connect with Catherine at:
- **Facebook Group:** Kingdom Treasures For Love, Finance, Family
- **Instagram:** @AlstonKingdom
- **Email:** Info@grantalston.com
- **Website:** www.grantalston.com
- **LinkedIn:** Catherine Latoya Grant Alston

Reginald Alston Jr.

Reginald Alston Jr. is the co-Founder of ART Financial Solutions, LLC, d/b/a Alston Kingdom, specializing in personal and business financial coaching, strategic vision planning, and treasury technology for corporations. ART Financial Solutions, LLC services the community and educational organizations by providing financial literacy, coaching, and training through the Alston Kingdom lifestyle brand.

After graduating from Southern Connecticut State University with a Bachelor of Arts, Reggie spent the next 14+ years as a trusted IT project management expert. He currently serves as a certified SCRUM Master (CSM) senior consultant at Slalom Consulting where he advises multiple clients throughout the region about strategy and deployment.

Reggie is a passionate and active member of the community. He holds a life membership in Kappa Alpha Psi Fraternity, Inc., where he serves on the executive board for the local chapter. He promotes diversity and inclusion by facilitating thought-provoking workshops for corporations within the New England area.

Reggie and his wife, Catherine, have two beautiful children and live in Connecticut.

You can connect with Reginald at:
- **Facebook Group:** Kingdom Treasures For Love, Finance, Family
- **Instagram:** @AlstonKingdom
- **LinkedIn:** Reginald Alston Jr
- **Website:** www.alstonkingdom.com

Tangie
McDougald

Tangie R. McDougald is a native of Hartford, Connecticut. She earned her Bachelor's degree in psychology and sociology from the University of Hartford and her Master's degree in clinical mental health counseling from the University of St. Joseph. She is a certified trauma-focused therapist and crisis worker.

Tangie remains on a mission to reduce the stigma for people of color who need behavioral health services. In 2017, she became the founder and CEO of Community Matters, LLC, a group practice that provides behavioral health services for adults. In 2020, she founded Community Matters Outpatient Psychiatric Clinic for Children where she remains the CEO. The clinic services children ages 5 to 18.

As an industry leader, she is vested in normalizing Black business bosses in the behavioral health field. Tangie provides counseling, coaching and consulting services to clinical professionals who are seeking to open or expand their practice. She is a member of Theta Alpha Sigma Alumnae Chapter of Sigma Gamma Rho Sorority Incorporated and a philanthropist, serving as the Community Service Chair for her sorority and as a clinical subject matter expert on the Black Network Channel. Tangie is a lifetime member of the NAACP and board member of the Scholarship Committee at The Town and Country Club. Tangie is a 2x best-selling author, wife, mother, and Glam-Ma of two amazing boys. Tangie understands what it takes to be a social change agent. She states, "It's personal," and stands firmly in the sisterhood of "Greater Service, Greater Progress."

You can connect with Tangie at: https://communitymattersopcc.com
- **Facebook Group** @Clinician to CEO
- **Instagram** @iamtangie_LPC
- **LinkedIn:** Tangie R. McDougald, NCC, LPC

Consults for clinicians, free discovery call: https://calendly.com/iamtangie

Kyle Lamar
McDougald

Kyle McDougald was born and raised in Hartford, Connecticut, and moved to Florida for several years before making his way back home. He has been employed with Colt's Manufacturing Co. for 10 years and is the vice-chair for Community Matters Outpatient Psychiatric Clinic for Children.

Kyle has a passion for helping others and spends his time assisting seniors and youth. He is a God-fearing man and well-known in his community for his skills as a barber. He enjoys connecting with others, traveling, riding his motorcycle, and spending time with his wife and family.

You can connect with Kyle on:
- **Facebook:** @KyleMcDougald
- **Instagram:** @Kyle McDougald
- **Website:** www.communitymattersoppc.com

Lashonda
Wofford

Lashonda Wofford is a wife, mother, sister, grandmother, friend, and a proven CEO. She has founded and built several successful organizations, including an affirmation collection, L&S Consulting Group, and Wofford & Williams Inc. d/b/a Akins Helping Hands. She is a community advocate and personal development partner who encourages everyone to bet on themselves through her All Bets on Me platform on Facebook.

Through various pains and struggles, Lashonda has learned to bet on herself and accomplish her goals despite adversities. She is a successful businesswoman of color who breaks the ceiling and creates tables for other women to have the same opportunities as she has. Some of Lashonda's noteworthy accomplishments are serving in the following roles: accredited certified instructor for Purpose Zeal Academy, certified executive leadership coach, certified life recovery coach, and certified mental health counselor.

She is also a 4x time best-selling author for the anthology project, *Blessed Not Broken, Vol. I*, her solo project *Pain Equals Purpose*, anthology *Igniting Your Purpose* and *90 Days of Biblical Affirmations for Christian Women in Business and Ministry*, all of which can be purchased through Amazon. She is the recipient of the 2022 ACHI Award for Public Service.

You can connect with Lashonda:
- All Bets On Me
- All Things Coaching

Travis Wofford

Travis Wofford is a multi-faceted businessman. He is the co-founder, president and CEO of Wofford and Williams Inc, the parent company of Akins Helping Hands, a company that provides healthcare resources to those in need.

Travis grew up in Pittsboro, NC, where he graduated from Northwood High School. He continued his education at Guilford Tech in Greensboro, NC. He now resides in Hope Mills, NC, where he enjoys listening to music and spending time with his devoted wife and family.

His YouTube Channel, The Average Man, serves as a platform for men to come together and discuss topics affecting them in today's society. Travis also actively uplifts and serves Black men and boys in his community by mentoring at-risk youth.

Because he understands the importance of creating jobs for black and brown people, Travis dreams of becoming a bestselling author and building a successful media and entertainment company. He works diligently to ensure Akins Helping Hands continues to grow by providing excellent, quality care to those in need.

You can connect with Mr. Wofford at:
- **Facebook**: Travis Wofford
- **Instagram**: twofford902
- **TikTok**: twofford902
- **YouTube**: Chopping It Up With The Wofford's

Dr. Sh'nai Simmons

Dr. Sh'nai Simmons is a licensed mental health counselor, clinical supervisor, and the co-founder of The Collective Wellness Institute, a private group mental health practice committed to providing superior services virtually and in person. Many counselors who have found themselves under the mentorship and direction of Dr. Sh'nai have benefited from her rich and diverse background. She has authored several books including collaborative projects, her solo testimonial, and a wellness planner, all of which are designed to inspire and facilitate wellness.

Dr. Sh'nai has a Master's degree in Community Counseling and a Doctorate in Counselor Education and Supervision from Regent University. She is an accomplished public speaker, trainer, and kingdom activist.

Mother of many children—two biological, two adopted, and countless spiritual—Dr. Sh'nai works closely in ministry with her husband, Taiwan Simmons, to build bridges. Together they labor to reinforce the power, purpose, and passion of traditional marriages through the Get in Touch Network. This power couple also fills community gaps through their nonprofit organization, Inside Reach Ministries.

You can connect with Dr. Sh'nai
- @DrShnai
- GetInTouchNetwork
- DrsNotes
- CommunityVictory

Websites:
www.Dr.Shnai.com
www.PlayfueledMarriages.com
www.TheCollectiveWellnessInstitute.com

Pastor Taiwan Simmons

As a product of a broken home, Taiwan (Pastor Tai) learned early on in life that family is not always your biological parents. These experiences, including a near-death event, being in foster care and overcoming self-esteem issues at an early age, helped Taiwan develop a passion and a heart for people.

Taiwan's approach has been to be a solution to the growing needs in the community. He is an author, mentor, public speaker, and has served on the boards of several local organizations.

Taiwan earned his graduate certificate in entrepreneurship and management training through Dale Carnegie has his graduate certificate in entrepreneurship and management training through Dale Carnegie. It is through these skills and accomplishments and his love for God and people, that Pastor Tai has a meaningful impact on the lives of those he ministers to.

In 2018, the Get in Touch Network was birthed out of a passion to heal and strengthen marriages. Playfuelled Marriages, an initiative of the Get in Touch Network, focuses on using the power of play to help couples grow. As co-founder of The Collective Wellness Institute, Pastor Tai offers Christian counseling, marriage counseling services, and marriage intensives.

You can connect with Pastor Tai:
- GetInTouchNetwork
- CommunityVictory

Website:
    www.Playfueledmarriages.com
    www.TheCollectiveWellnessInstitute.com

Tamara Mitchell-Davis

Tamara Mitchell-Davis is a nine-time bestselling and award-winning author, wife, mother, and CEO of TM Davis Enterprises, LLC. She holds an MBA and an 085 School Business Administrator Certification from the State of Connecticut. Her published works include #GoalGetter: Strategies for Overcoming Life's Challenges; Goodbye Fear, Hello Destiny; Dream Your Plan, Plan Your Dream: 7 Steps to Manifesting Success; Blessed Not Broken (Vols.1, 2, 3, 4 and 5) and coauthor in Dear Momma. She is the founder of the Pen to Profit: Write, Publish & Build community on Facebook, the host of the annual Pen to Profit Conference, and the creator and host of The CEO Wife Experience Podcast.

Tamara awards include: 100 Women of Color for leadership and community service; ACHI Magazine Orator of the Year; Women of Elevation Triumphant Author; I Am H.E.R International Woman on the Rise and CEO of the Year; and Phenomenal Woman In Business, to name a few.

Media appearances include Women of Distinction Magazine, Inquiring News, Making Headline News, Voyage Dallas Magazine, Voyage ATL Magazine, Canvas Rebel and Black Women Mean Business Magazine.

She is an active member of Delta Sigma Theta Sorority, Incorporated, and resides in Connecticut with her husband and their children.

You can connect with Tamara
- **Facebook:** theceowife
- **Instagram:** theceowife860
- **Email:** info@theceowife.com
- **Website**: www.theceowife.com
- **Facebook group**: https://bit.ly/P2PCOMMUNITY
- **LinkedIN:** Tamara Mitchell-Davis

Joe Davis

Joe Davis was born in Rhode Island but grew up and lived the majority of his life in Hartford, Connecticut. His love for basketball was the foundation of JD Enterprises LLC. He fulfilled his mission to bring Ruckers-style basketball to the inner city with a successful league of teams for both youth and adults. Joe and his coaches, players, officials, and supporters promoted positivity, teamwork, and the importance of community. He is an avid sports fan and loves following the Pittsburgh Steelers (NFL) and the Los Angeles Lakers (NBA).

Joe is a God-fearing man who loves his wife, children, and family. He enjoys listening to music and spending time at home. His goal is to become a bestselling author and eventually write his own life story.

Joe resides in Connecticut with his wife, family, and their puppy.

www.ingramcontent.com/pod-product-compliance
Lightning Source LLC
Chambersburg PA
CBHW072056110526
44590CB00018B/3197